MW00877654

Diary

of a

Racer's Wife

Susie,
    Every life is a ~~journey~~. I'm
blessed that you are part of mine,
and pray the Lord's favor over
you & your family.
              Gayle

Gayle Kott

Diary of a Racer's Wife

Copyright © 2018 by Gayle Kott
All rights reserved
ISBN: 1545534608
ISBN-13: 9781545534601

To my boys
Zeke, Andy, Jason and Chris
Who grew up racing
You've become fine men
And I'm proud of you

Diary of a Racer's Wife

Table of Contents

Diary of a Racer's Wife

Diary of a Racer's Wife

Prologue

The boulder gained speed as it rolled down the hillside, heading straight toward the highway and our car. I knew Fritz saw it too, and was gauging how fast he had to go to get us out of harm's way – since we were in the 'speed stage' of the race, he was already pushing the limit of what was safe, especially considering we had the youngest of our three children in the car with us. I knew if it hit us, even with the protection of the Lincoln and its roll cage, we would likely end up splattered all over that Mexican highway. I couldn't help but wonder who would go to all the trouble to do this – that boulder was huge, and getting it started on its downhill trajectory must have been no small task. I was fairly sure it wasn't personal - they apparently just wanted to create or see some carnage. I also couldn't help but wonder as I watched it bounce closer: how in the world did a girl like me end up in a place like this?

Diary of a Racer's Wife

Chapter 1

The Stuff Legends Are Made Of

I met my husband at the Bonneville Salt Flats during Speed Week, August 1985. While the vast majority of the racers I know are genuinely good people, they are focused on one thing during racing season – speed. And Fritz Kott was exceptionally focused in that area – to be the fastest with whatever he had to work with. Model A, old Harley, go-kart, or anything else with an engine, he would do whatever he could to get just a little more out of it, no matter what it took.

Fritz was one of those people who spent their entire lives with machines. He understood them far better than he understood people – he told me once that machines could never hurt him the way people could. Fritz's love affair with the mechanical began at a very young age. He told me when he was about eight or nine, he and little sister Jeanie would take his wagon down to the salvage yard. There they collected pieces of a scrapped aircraft they called the 'U.S.S. Catfish' in order to set up his own personal WWII fighter in their back yard. He even convinced their mom to take her Chrysler to the scrap yard to get a few of the larger items, like a piece of the cowl, which she loaded into the trunk. Of course, he didn't end up with an entire airplane, but there were enough bits and pieces for him to keep Balboa Island safe for democracy, at least in his imagination.

That was also about the age when his dad, Lonnie,

4

first taught him to drive, in a 1915 Model T truck. His parents divorced in the mid '50's, and he divided his time between his mother in Whittier and his father in Newport Beach. Lonnie owned and operated Newport Plating. While at Newport, Fritz and his friends experimented with building rafts, rowing around the bay in skiffs, and in general loving the ocean. As a teenager and young man he worked for his dad at the plating shop. Not only did he learn about that industry, he met a number of celebrities who had boats or homes in either Newport or Balboa, including Dan Blocker (Hoss from Bonanza) and John Wayne. My favorite of his stories was about John Wayne.

Fritz was helping Mr. Wayne with his boat and they were discussing some sort of problem with someone – I was never entirely clear on exactly what the problem was. According to Fritz, Mr. Wayne said, "Well maybe I'd better go get my six shooter and we'd better go have a little talk with them." I somehow doubt they actually followed through with that course of action, but Fritz was nonetheless delighted at the Hollywood star's response. He told me that he didn't think Mr. Wayne was acting in the movies – that's who he really was.

Although Fritz's father remarried twice, his mother Charlsey never did, so Fritz did his best to look after her. When he was in fifth grade, her '41 Chrysler blew a head gasket. Fritz hopped on his bicycle, rode down to the gas station, bought a head gasket for $1.50, and went home and changed it for her. I know raising Fritz was a challenge for Charlsey, because she told me it was. The neighbors weren't always pleased with the accumulation of what they perceived as junk, but what Fritz perceived as treasure. This was a theme that would follow him throughout his life, and one he could never understand.

In sixth grade he was the only kid in the neighborhood to have a ported and relieved lawnmower engine

5

in his go-kart. Go-karting on the streets of Whittier was frowned on in the '50's by the local police, and they would frequently give chase. On at least one occasion, Fritz and go-kart went flying around the corner, saw the open garage door of a neighbor, drove inside and pulled the door down after him. The police screamed around the corner in hot pursuit, but neither Fritz nor go-kart were anywhere to be seen. They cruised up and down the block a bit trying to figure out where he had gone until they finally decided they had more important things to do. Fritz waited a few minutes, listening intently for any movement, before peering cautiously out of the garage. Then, seeing the coast was clear, he continued on his way home.

While in the 7th grade, his paper route money was saved for buying his first car, a Model A Ford, which he and his friends pushed around Whittier because he was too young to have a license. By the time he was in High School he also had a Model T. He said he did it backwards – had the Model A first, and then a Model T. He used to drive the Model T to school, and one morning while getting ready to leave it popped into gear while he was cranking the starter, and it chased him across the street and pinned him against his neighbor's garage.

As soon as he had his license he started running the Long Beach Model T Hill Climb at Signal Hill. He built a wooden speedster body for his T, and was a frequent winner in his class. For some reason a number of the older guys competing at the hill climb weren't too crazy about Fritz, especially when he would beat them. On one occasion a couple of them decided that his T was too fast and must have a Model C crankshaft, which would have been illegal. They agonized over this for a little while, but finally decided to put up the $20 fee to protest him. The purpose of the protest process was to keep racers honest regarding the parts they were using. The purpose of the $20 was to prevent frivolous protests from occurring, and provide the racer, if innocent, with the funding for a replacement gasket. Keep in mind $20 went a lot further in the '60's than it does now. Fritz, not wanting to crawl under the car to remove the pan, had a couple of his buddies help him lay it on its side onto some K-rail. He proceeded to pull the pan, show the judges his stock T crank and collect his money. After he'd had enough fun with the other competitors complaining about his wooden speedster going so fast, he put an extremely rusty and dilapidated Model T touring body on the chassis. He still won his division, which further irritated the grumbling racers.

It's fairly amazing that Fritz's sense of humor didn't get him into more trouble than it did. One rainy evening he and some friends were doing donuts in his buddy's Volkswagen in a very muddy cornfield in Santa Fe Springs. The local police had driven their cruiser into the cornfield after them to reprimand the culprits. The cops didn't really want to get out of their car in the rain, so they seemed somewhat relieved when the young men got out of their vehicle to speak with them. This was definitely a more trusting era. What they didn't realize was that their heavy cruiser was sinking up to its axles in the mud. Fritz noticed, though, and had an idea. While his buddy was at the window trying to convince the officers what fine, upstanding citizens they were, Fritz surreptitiously scooped up several large handfuls of mud and placed them on the top of the police car near the front. As the rain continued to fall, the mud began oozing down over the windshield, effectively covering it. The teenagers jumped in their light weight VW - no doubt with the tire pressure already lowered to keep them from getting stuck - and took off, leaving the disgruntled policemen spinning their tires and sinking deeper into the mud.

Another time he and his friend Randy were riding

their BSAs around the freshly resurfaced track at Whittier College. They both did some flat track racing, and it seemed like a good test track, although the college administration no doubt had a different point of view. A motorcycle cop on a big full-dress Harley started to chase them, so Fritz and his buddy just rode their stripped-down bikes straight up the nearby hill, and sat there watching the officer unsuccessfully try to follow them. After watching a number of futile attempts, they felt sorry for the guy, not to mention they were concerned that he might dump the bike with his efforts, and rode back down to talk to him. The officer told them it was a good thing they had come back or they would have been in big trouble. Fritz and Randy knew that he never could have caught them, but humored him and apologized, being let go with a warning.

And then there was the swimming pool incident. Fritz and some of his friends decided to go swimming after hours in the pool at Whittier High. Naturally, the school was locked, so the group decided to try climbing the wall near the pool and jumping off into the water. According to Fritz, he decided that as he was probably in the best condition he would be the first one to try it and see how plausible it was. He took a deep breath, jumped out as far as he could, and still scraped the side of the pool as he hit the water. As soon as he surfaced he yelled up to his friends, "Don't try that!" Undaunted, they all managed to get in another way and had a wonderful time.

Fritz loved his dog Sam, a big German Shepherd. Even though a number of the neighbors were afraid of him, Fritz refused to tie up the dog. He finally got arrested for violating the leash law after a neighbor complained. Charlsey didn't ingratiate herself to the judge when she quoted the television show "Laugh In" when the judge entered the court room, saying "Here come da judge, here come da judge. Order in da court cause here come da judge." Fritz ended up going to jail for a few days, but managed to get released a day early so he could go to the Antique Nationals, which is a story the announcer recounted nearly every year he attended.

Having been raised in part near the ocean, he loved diving and fishing and surfing. During one trip to Mexico, he and a couple of buddies decided to experiment fishing with some dynamite he had found in an abandoned gold mine. Yes, he took dynamite with him into Mexico. No, it was not the first time. And yes, it was probably not the wisest thing he ever did, but it always worked out for him. The idea was the explosion would stun the fish in the bay, and he and his friends could collect them at their leisure.

He lit the fuse and pitched the stick of dynamite behind their rowboat. The guys frantically started rowing to get out of range before it blew. There was one problem with this. The floating dynamite got caught in the wake of the boat, and just kept following them, no matter how hard they pulled on the oars. Not rowing, however, didn't seem like a good plan either, as the fuse was growing inexorably shorter. The resulting explosion capsized the boat – I'm not sure how far it or the guys flew into the air before hitting the water. Once they all resurfaced and collected the oars, and their wits, they decided to gather some of the fish that had been brought up. Fritz saw one really big fin rise to the surface. As whatever it belonged to was larger than their boat, he was relieved when it kind of shook itself after a moment, and submerged back into the depths. While there were a lot of other more manageable fish that had been stunned, they would regain their senses and swim off, right as the boat was approaching. I'm pretty sure the group all ended up eating tacos that night, as Fritz and his buddies were unable to capture any of the elusive fish. It was an experience for them, but one that they had the sense not to repeat.

Diary of a Racer's Wife

It had seemed like a good idea at the time, but it wasn't a particularly productive way to catch dinner.

In the early '60's Fritz enlisted in the Army reserve. While he was stationed at Fort Ord in northern California, he managed to talk his sergeant into letting him keep his 1954 Harley K Model up there so he could ride AMA District 37 races on weekends. The sergeant, also a motorcycle enthusiast, agreed, as he thought it would be good public relations, and offered to store the Harley for Fritz.

He also became good friends with the mess sergeant, especially after a visit from the inspector general early on in Fritz's military career. The men were lined up at attention and had been instructed to answer any questions the I.G. might ask "Yes, sir" "No, sir". The I.G. went down the line, stopping occasionally to ask one of the men a question. He happened to stop at Fritz and asked if he was being treated well. Fritz responded that he was treated very well except they didn't give him enough to eat. At the next meal his company commander took him by one arm and his sergeant by the other and they proceeded to march him down the chow line, making sure he got double portions of everything, then sat with him and made sure he ate every bite of it. For Fritz, this was no problem. He loved food, and one of his mottos was: "Full is no excuse." Between that, and the fact that Fritz actually enjoyed K.P. duty, the mess sergeant let him have extra food whenever he wanted it.

Fritz never saw active duty, but he and his company were sent to keep peace during the Watts riots. He scraped his nose on his helmet jumping out of the back of the military deuce and a half truck, but his greater concern was that none of the soldiers were given real bullets for their M-1s. He was pretty sure some of the people rioting had real bullets for their guns, so he chose not to point his at anyone, as that seemed more prudent.

10

When he wasn't riding in AMA District 36 and 37 events, Fritz was devoted to drag racing. He called his Model A roadster pickup, The Full House Mouse, the most raced Model A roadster in the world. He ran at all the southwestern big name tracks of the day – Lyons, Irwindale, Orange County, Paradise Mesa, Tijuana, etc. One particular time at Colton he made it to the finals in his roadster pickup, powered by a flathead Ford V8 engine that he had built, running against a Hell's Angel on his Harley. Fritz knew that discretion was the better part of valor in this case and common sense would dictate throwing the race. He intended to do this until about half track, when he couldn't help putting his foot in the throttle and edging the Angel out. After the race, he pulled into his pit and started draining the water out of his radiator, which was a standard procedure at the end of the race day, especially with a flathead. He looked up a saw a swarm of Hell's Angels heading towards him and thought, "Oh man, here we go," and he and his friends braced themselves for what they thought would be the ensuing fight.

As the motorcycle gang surrounded the roadster pickup, he was extremely relieved to hear them say, "Hey man, what do you have in this thing? That was great!" So, Fritz proceeded to show them and tell them about his engine. He probably didn't mention that he built a lot of Harley engines for the Hessians, one of their rival gangs.

Fritz also did some oval track racing, running midgets and TQs – three quarter midgets – at Pearsonville and Ascot. I don't know much about that part of his racing life, other than he was reasonably successful and enjoyed it, but it wasn't the passion that Dry Lakes racing became. He did nearly cry - literally- when he found out Ascot was being torn down, however.

As I said, Dry Lakes racing was one of Fritz's true passions. He started out with the Forever Fours when

11

Diary of a Racer's Wife

they held their one-eighth mile drags at El Mirage Dry Lake in the Mojave Desert in the late '60's. His first trip to Bonneville was in about 1970 with his friend Dick. There is no ambivalence about Bonneville – you either love it or hate it. Fritz loved it, and he loved it for the rest of his life. I believe it was land speed racing legend Fred Lobello who gave him his first rule book, which he poured over. The next season Fritz had his Model A roadster pickup, the Full House Mouse, on the salt, with what was to become an almost iconic number in that community, 408. He chose 408 because sometimes he would run a four cylinder Ford engine, commonly referred to as a "four banger", or a flathead Ford V-8 engine - 4 Or 8. He also started running the roadster pickup at SCTA (Southern California Timing Association) events at El Mirage. Various friends and relatives would tow him back from the other end of the course after he passed the timing stand. He used to joke about how Ralph, his brother-in-law at the time, would beat him to the finish line in the support vehicle – Ralph's souped up El Camino. Bear in mind that Fritz was running pretty consistently around 100 mph in the Model A. Stories about Fritz towing burning VW cases and flaming tires around the lake bed on Saturday night before Sunday's races became the stuff of local legend. This type of thing would be frowned upon now, to say the least, but it seemed like the thing to do at the time.

During this period, Fritz had been married twice, and before 1985, divorced twice. And then I came into the picture, a fairly conservative young woman originally from the Midwest, with a young son, who was going through a divorce of her own.

Chapter 2

Salt Flats and Sea Lions

My first marriage had recently ended under less than ideal circumstances, and when my sister Sally offered me and my four-year-old son Andy the opportunity to go to Speed Week with her, her fiancé Dick, and her two kids, Stacey and David, I jumped at the chance. I had maintained an interest in racing since I was about five when my Dad took me to a stock car race at the local fairgrounds (I remember telling him when I grew up I was going to do that) so, having heard of Bonneville as a Mecca of racing, it seemed like a good idea.

As we were getting to the Salt Flats, Dick mentioned that we would probably see his friend Fritz there, and warned me that "He can fix your car, but don't fall in love with him". Well, I didn't have a car at the time, so...

The first time I saw Fritz, he was wearing fluorescent orange swimming trunks, no shirt, wrap-around sunglasses that weren't particularly flattering, and was flying around a corner in the pits on a skateboard, being towed by his seemingly daredevil four-year-old son Zeke on a Honda ATC70. After learning who he was, I turned to Sally and said, "Tell Dick not to worry, he (Fritz) is not my type." Make no mistake, it wasn't about his physical appearance. Fritz was about 6'1", well built, with wavy blondish brown hair and blue eyes, and had a deep golden tan from working in the sun all his life. I just felt he was a bit too flamboyant for my taste.

13

Diary of a Racer's Wife

For those of you who have never been there, Bonneville is a unique place. Created millennia ago by an inland sea, it stretches for miles near the western border of Utah along Interstate 80, flat and glaringly white. People have lost their way and died of dehydration, heat stroke and the like. And I don't mean just back in the old days - I know of a couple who lost their lives there in that way after the turn of the current century. Sudden violent electrical storms come up and turn the hard, dry salt into a corrosive quagmire. It is not a place to be taken lightly, but it is most definitely one of the best places on earth to go fast.

Neither Fritz nor Dick were campaigning anything of their own that meet, so I spent the week as a spectator and trying to keep enough sunscreen on my young son and myself. The salt reflects the sunlight back up at you, and places that don't normally burn, like the underside of your chin, can become very painful if left unprotected. The first night we set up camp in the gravel pits a few miles from the salt. No one is allowed to stay on the salt overnight during Speed Week for security reasons. Fritz and Zeke were camping with us, and when we first established our campsite, Fritz took a can of black spray paint out of the back of his '60 Chevy pickup, painted a 2'x 2' square on the ground and wrote the word "BAD" in it. He said, "Now this is the bad box. If anyone is bad, they have to come and stand in it." So, being a bit of a smart aleck, I hung my head and went over to stand in the box. Fritz laughed and said, "Well, I actually meant it for the kids, but I'll take care of you later."

Dinner that night was supposed to be macaroni and cheese and hot dogs. I realize this shouldn't have been too complicated, but we were working on the tailgate of a truck in the dark with an old Coleman stove that wouldn't boil water at our elevation, over 4,000 feet. After we decided the water was never going to come to a boil, Sally and I thought we'd go ahead and put the macaroni in anyway. Now, I don't know if you've ever tried this, but if you haven't, don't. Why we didn't have a flashlight, a lantern, or some form of light, I can't say, but we let it cook for a while in the darkness until we decided it had to be done, and took it in front of the headlights to drain it. Instead of clear water with nicely cooked macaroni being caught against the lid, we were draining this white pasty goo. So, we used the glare of the headlights to look in the pot and that's all there was - no macaroni, just white pasty goo. Having several hungry children and not a lot of options, we went ahead and added the cheese sauce and added sliced up hotdogs. Fritz took one look and said, "Do you know what that's going to do to the inside of your stomach?" and proceeded to try to heat up a can of menudo which he had brought for his dinner.

The grease floating on the top of it wouldn't even melt, so I looked at it and said, "Do you know what that's going to do to the inside of *your* stomach?" and continued eating my cheesy hot dog goo. We all ate breakfast in town at a casino the next morning, which was a very good choice. Andy and I sat with Fritz and Zeke, and Fritz and I began to form a friendship. At the end of Speed Week, Fritz and Dick decided to caravan back to Southern California together.

Since we were on vacation, Dick wanted to come back through Yosemite National Park. This was a wonderful idea to me, as I had never been there. While looking for a campsite, we came upon one with a half dozen late model Japanese motorcycles nearby, and Dick said something to the effect of, "Oh, looks like we've got the Hell's Angels here, we'd better find another site." So, we drove on a little further.

Having finally established camp, Fritz and I decided

15

Diary of a Racer's Wife

to take a hike. On our way, we came across the guys with the bikes, who were in their early twenties and about as clean cut as Wally Cleaver. When we told them what Dick had said, they started laughing and one guy said, "I gotta go call my Mom and tell her." The real reason I mention the Yosemite part of the trip, however, is that on that hike, inside a hollow redwood tree which was lying on its side, which we called the tunnel tree, Fritz first kissed me. It was one of those long, passionate kisses that girls read about in romance novels. I was falling hard.

After we got back to Southern California, Fritz thought it was ridiculous that I didn't have any transportation, which was a side effect of my broken first marriage. Since that was completely unacceptable to him, he decided to buy me a little Chevy Luv truck. It needed some work, but I soon learned that was not a problem for him. Fritz could fix anything mechanical, and I mean anything. He had a gift - there is no other way to describe it. If he couldn't find parts for something, he would make them. If he needed a tool he didn't have or couldn't get, he would make it. He was amazing. But to get back to the truck, it took me a bit to get used to driving with a manual transmission again, however it wasn't long before I was regularly driving from my apartment in San Bernardino down to Fritz's ten acre property outside of Fallbrook, known by family and friends as "the ranch."

In early September, Fritz asked me if I wanted to go to the Reno Air Races with him to spectate. Being a fan of aircraft since I was a kid, I jumped at the chance. Andy was with his dad that weekend, but we picked up Zeke from his mother near Santa Cruz and drove to Reno, camping out in the back of the '60 Chevy pickup. We had a great time. I remember getting to meet World War II ace Greg "Pappy" Boyington, and in general thoroughly enjoying the races. Sleeping in a truck has its disadvan-

16

tages, though, one of them being bathing, or rather, the lack thereof. So, on the way back to Santa Cruz we pulled off next to the Truckee River to clean up a bit. I wasn't about to meet Fritz's ex-wife, Evie, feeling gungy and with dirty hair. For those of you that don't know, most of the water in the Truckee is the result of the snow runoff from the Sierra Nevada Mountains. It remains the coldest bath I've had to date, but it was good to be clean again.

After dropping Zeke off at his mom's, we spent the night and the following day in Monterey. It was then that I knew I had found the one for me, even if he did converse with the sea lions at the wharf and on the beach. Maybe partially *because* he conversed with sea lions. He did a remarkable imitation of a sea lion's bark. He must have said something offensive in sea lion, though, because a big male on the beach was obviously annoyed by something in the conversation. After spending the day in town, we decided to take the 17 Mile Drive into Carmel, which was lovely. Fritz surprised me with a bottle of champagne and some smoked oysters. This was to compensate for the night before - we had come into Monterey on fumes, with less than ten dollars to buy food. I was assured that this would be corrected in the morning when his bank opened. Meanwhile, we were contemplating the best way to spend those ten dollars, and a two dollar bottle of wine held a certain appeal for me. Fritz vetoed it, though, saying, "Nothing but champagne for you, baby." Yeah, I knew it was a hokey line, but I still liked it, and we spent the money on more sensible things, like almond cookies.

It was also in September of '85 that I attended my first El Mirage dry lakes meet. As I've said, El Mirage is a dry lake bed in the Mojave where the Southern California Timing Association holds time trials six times a year. The race vehicle - whether it be a stock bodied car or motorcycle, or something more modified, like a competition

17

coupe, lakester, streamliner, etc.- is timed on a dedicated course over 1.3 miles, with about a mile of shut down area. Speeds can range from around 50 mph for small displacement motorcycles to over 300 mph for some of the streamliners and lakesters. Fritz wasn't running anything that meet, so he basically showed me around and introduced me to people. At least, he introduced me when he could remember my name - we were engaged for about six months before he got it right on a regular basis. "This is my fiancé uh..uh.. [elbow in the ribs] Gayle." Sometimes I wondered if he did it just to mess with me - it's hard to say. When I first met him he didn't know how old he was. I thought it was just vanity, saying he was 39 instead of 40, but soon found out he genuinely hadn't done the math, and didn't know. He said he had too much important stuff in his brain to crowd it with that type of information.

We had decided to run the Harley at the November El Mirage meet, so we went to Santa Cruz to bring Zeke down to the desert for the weekend. Now, most people think of deserts as being hot and dry. El Mirage in November is still usually dry, at least when you're lucky, but definitely not hot, especially after dark. So, there we were on Saturday night, the temperature being 17 degrees, teeth chattering, trying to sleep in the back of Fritz's trusty '60 Chevy pickup covered by a camper shell without a back window, with Zeke in between us in the sleeping bags to keep him warm. Zeke piped up, "Boy, Dad, isn't this the life?" and we had to agree.

Chapter 3

Lincolns and Learning Curves

Over the winter, Fritz heard about a vintage road race down in Baja, Mexico, called the La Carrera Classic. He had recently purchased a 1954 Lincoln Capri Coupe, which was ideal for that type of event. I admit, when I first saw the car, I wasn't particularly fond of it. It was yellow with a black top, and a yellow and black car had for some obscure reason frightened me when I was a young child. All of my misgivings went away after he let me drive it. That car was very comfortable and handled exceptionally well. We weren't sure we wanted to spend the money on the actual entry fee (spending money wasn't Fritz's vice) so we and our friend Jim T. decided to drive down to Ensenada with his son Michael and our sons Andy and Zeke, and we would all basically "follow the pack" in the Lincoln.

Fritz put a lot of work into the Lincoln before the race, to the exclusion of everything else. He was self-employed at the time, so he just kind of quit working for people, which really annoyed a couple of them, not to mention the electric company, phone company, etc. He also decided to make the car look more like the old Pan American road race Lincolns from the 1950's, and added some "temporary"graphics.

When we got down to Ensenada, the organizers of the event didn't quite know what to make of us at first. For one thing, the competitors there had some seriously expensive iron (aluminum?) including Ferarris, Bugattis, a Mercedes Gull Wing, etc. and were staying in what is considered a nice resort. We stayed in the parking lot, sleeping in our car, a theme which would recur in our racing career. For another, we hadn't actually entered the race, but planned on running it anyway. But, Fritz had a way with people when he wanted to, and it wasn't long before he had convinced the powers that be that it would be just fine for us to do exactly what he wanted.

We followed the officially entered cars, enjoying the drive, although with his family in the car Fritz didn't feel it was prudent to exceed 110 mph or so. The race stretched 120 miles from outside Ensenada to the other side of Baja California ending up in San Felipe. We camped that night on the beach in San Felipe, sleeping bags rolled out on the sand.

When I woke up in the morning there was Fritz, not curled up around me, but facing the other way with his arm over a skinny brown stray dog that had cuddled up next to him for warmth during the night. Jim thought it was about the funniest thing he'd ever seen. I think it can still bring a chuckle when he thinks about it. While Jim continued to laugh about the dog, we packed our belongings into the Lincoln and talked about the race. Fritz genuinely enjoyed the its layout, and before we left Mexico he was already making plans for officially participating the following year.

My first experience with being part of a racing team at Bonneville that summer was a pretty sharp learning curve. Naturally, it began at home with preparing the '54 Harley - and I had thought he was obsessive about the Lincoln! Countless hours went into it, and the KH Harley itself had taken up residency in our living room while he worked on it. Once we got to the salt, I understood in general what was happening from my experiences the previous year. I just had to learn how to be a good crew chief without bending any rules that my rider didn't deem important enough to tell me about. Well, I'm sure he acknowledged their importance for most people, but sometimes I think he felt like he had been doing it so long that not everything should apply to him. I got my first lessons in towing and backing a trailer that year. I made another racer fairly nervous when I almost hit his race car, but missed it by at least a quarter of an inch. I was far better at figuring out how to safely navigate the return roads, which is another useful skill. Unfortunately, I didn't have the opportunity to learn about making return record runs. That was to be a lesson for another year.

Fritz was nearly always up for vintage drag racing, and I wanted to give it a try as well. I got my first opportunity at the Antique Drags in Carlsbad, in our '39 Ford standard coupe, powered by a '51 Oldsmobile engine. Fritz's biggest concern was that I was gentle with the transmission, as Lincoln Zephyr gears were hard to come by. Fritz knew the starter, Bob Higbee, who was also the chief starter for El Mirage, and explained that I was new to this and he wanted to ride with me to show me what to do. Bob, not only being a gentleman, but very sensible, allowed this.

So, there we were at the line. Fritz was always quite the showman. He told me to back up to do a burn out. I would have been happy to just make it to the other end without embarrassing myself, but readily agreed. He got out of the car and threw water under the back tires of both our car and the competition. He got back into the car and I revved the engine and smoked the tires, with the fans in the stands cheering.

As I returned to the staging lights, known as the Christmas tree, I wasn't exactly smooth with the clutch and the car lurched toward the lights like a stumbling drunk - ka-thunk, ka- thunk, ka-thunk. Well, at least I didn't stall it, or break any gears in the transmission. The crowd erupted again, this time with laughter. I staged the car, and took off with the green. I don't remember my reaction time, although I doubt it was stellar. I didn't win the race, but, staging aside, I made a clean pass and at least learned the basics of how it was done. I'm sure it was the most original burn out of the day. I overheard a couple of guys talking about it, okay, maybe they were laughing about it, at the following El Mirage meet.

It was also at Carlsbad that I first started learning a bit more about Fritz's past. A lady he didn't know came up to us, looked at him for a moment, and said, "I remember you from Irwindale!" Fritz instantly knew what she meant. It seems back in the '70's he and his friend Greg had decided to 'streak' down the drag strip at Irwindale during a break between races. I have to admit, I was kind of surprised she recognized him with his clothes on. Well, at least he had the physique for it.

It was at the September '86 El Mirage meet that we set our first record together with the K Model. There was a minimum in the class of 125, which we exceeded by less than a mile per hour, but enough to get the record. We were so happy! The competition in our class, who was running a Triumph, had some minor mechanical issues, and they were going to pack up and go home. Fritz thought that was a shame, so he helped them out, supplying them with what they needed, and they were able to make another run, breaking our brand new record.

We were at the starting line when we heard the news. Fritz had just helped them get off the line, and I looked at him and, half joking, shouted, "And you fixed their bike!" and kicked my flip flop toward him. I didn't actually mean for it to leave my right foot, but it flew about ten feet into the air, sailing directly past a starting

21

Diary of a Racer's Wife

line official, as well as a handful of other innocent by-standers. I realize that was not one of my finest moments - Fritz had done the right thing, and I knew that. So, our first record together survived about an hour, but it gave us something to work toward - beating the new one.

Andy, Zeke, Gayle and Fritz
La Carrera Classic
Viva Mexico!

22

Chapter 4

"The Family that Honeymoons Together Eats Prunes Together"

In January, 1987, Burr Oxley, who was editor at the time of the Road Race Lincoln Register, called to offer financial support from the club in the amount of $250 if we wanted to compete in the La Carrera Classic again. Since this covered most of the entry fee, we gratefully accepted his offer, with the proviso that I write an article for the publication on our adventures. From that point on, our lives revolved more and more around the upcoming road race. We carefully researched the correct graphics for the car. A friend of ours from Ohio, Rick, loaned us a couple of his "Hot Rod" magazines from the '50's and gave us a video tape of the 1954 Mexican Road Race. We watched it so many times I can still hear the narrator's voice in my head three decades later: "Mexico, with her wide skies and ancient churches. With her people isolated from the uneasy age of the atom, following old ways, tuned to the tempo of a donkey's patient pace..."

Neither Fritz nor I were what you would call professional artists, but with his perfectionism and my patience we were finally able to get the car looking somewhat presentable in its "road race regalia." Which was good, because I had begun seeing Mobil Oil's flying red horse and Mexican and American crossed flags in my sleep. Naturally, Fritz wanted to make the car run as well as it looked. He replaced the 'teapot' Holley Carburetor with a

23

Holley 1850 four barrel, which we bought at a speed shop for $99 - that was definitely the deal of the day. We were going to put in a cam and lifters, but the cam didn't get ground in time, so we ran with what we had. The suspension was a bit more of an issue than the engine. The front shocks were so bad that if you hit a dip at more than five miles per hour you would bounce for two blocks. We tried three different types of shocks before our friend Jim located a pair of Monroe '56 Ford pickup shocks, which had the same part number as Lincoln, for three bucks for the pair. These finally did the trick. We also added some spring spacers to the front springs and installed an inexpensive pair of Lakewood traction bars to stabilize the rear end. The total price for our suspension modifications was around $25.00. We also made a few modifications to the engine, including porting the intake manifold, as Fritz was very skilled at port matching. He also created a way to install dual exhaust on the car, which, with the space limitations in the engine compartment was a bit of a challenge, to say the least. A major pain in the neck, to say the most.

   We were finally as ready as we were going to be with the time we had left, which was none. Our friend Jim T. was going to be the co-driver, but at the last minute problems arose and he couldn't make it. Our support team members likewise cancelled at the last minute, which meant I had to be support crew instead of alternate co-driver. So, we loaded our '60 VW camper, grabbed the kids and the Lincoln, and took off for sunny Baja California. We arrived at Estero Beach around 11:30 am on Friday April 10th. There was a photojournalist who for some reason found our slightly bizarre looking modified camper and Lincoln fascinating. A photo of our camper and the Lincoln showed up in a French magazine a few months later with the caption "Snobs." I was never quite sure if he meant that as a joke, misinterpreted the word, or what, as it didn't remotely apply. "Redneck" would have perhaps been more appropriate.

Registration and tech inspection were supposed to begin at noon. While we were waiting, we used the time to work on more of the Lincoln's lettering. It took a bit to figure out where registration was going to happen and what was going on, which was okay because the officials were still trying to figure it out too. Hey, it wasn't NASCAR, it was Mexico.

We managed to get through registration and found a tech inspector. The purpose of technical inspection is to make sure the race vehicle and the driver's racing apparel are within safety specifications. Tech inspection at this event wasn't particularly overwhelming - the inspector just fondled the roll bar a little bit and checked the fire extinguisher and gave us the okay. That evening there was a car show and driver's meeting at the Community Center in Ensenada. Aside from us, there was only one other car painted in full road race style, a '55 Austin Healey. Granted, a few others had made a slight attempt, but hadn't gotten carried away as much as we had. Of course if my car had held the value of some of theirs I might have had second thoughts about it myself. Not Fritz, though. He still would have painted it road race style, no matter what it was.

The variety of cars ran from Ferraris to Allards to Morgans, with the occasional Lancia or Bugatti thrown in for good measure. In our class we were competing against a '59 Edsel, a '63 Thunderbird, a '64 Mercury, a '70-ish Cadillac, a '53 Buick and a '56 Dodge D-500. At the actual meeting there were only a few points that became of real importance to us - that 112 octane racing gas and water would be available at the mandatory ten minute pit stop, and to go as fast as you wanted across the finish line.

Yeah. Right. We should have reminded ourselves again that it wasn't NASCAR, it was Mexico.

The rest of the evening and early the next morning were spent putting the finishing touches on the Lincoln. We spoke with Bill Stroppe quite extensively before the race, who was driving a flathead powered Kurtis. He reminisced about the days when he was preparing the original road race Lincolns in the early '50's, as well as giving us a little technical advice. We had been concerned about the valves floating at around 5000 rpm. He told us that in the original road race Lincolns they had been concerned about the same problem. They tried using Ford truck cam and lifters, but weren't satisfied with the performance, so they returned to the original Lincoln parts and let the valves float, which never actually caused a problem.

Finally it was time for the cars to head from Estero Beach to downtown Ensenada where the "false start" would be staged. This was basically a parade through town to give spectators a chance to see the cars and get into the "road race spirit". The real start of the race was at the 10 Kilometer marker on Highway 3 outside Ensenada. The cars left at one-minute intervals, supposedly with the fastest cars leaving first and progressing to the slowest cars. This was a good idea in theory, but theory and reality don't always coincide. They started our Lincoln about fourth from last. Actually, this was perfectly fine with Fritz because it gave him the added fun of being able to pass so many cars. Since Fritz had no co-driver and we weren't high tech enough back in the '80's to have a video camera, Fritz had to take 35 mm photos and man a cassette tape recorder en route. The purpose of the tape recorder was so he could talk about the course, the car, the conditions, whatever. We had done that the previous year, as well, and I figured it would be helpful in writing the article I had promised the Road Race Lincoln Register and our buddy Jim would want to hear it. It wasn't long after he left the starting line that Fritz started passing cars. The first section of the 120 mile course consists of winding mountain roads and tight turns. One of the cars had been painted up like a police car, complete with lights and sirens. Apparently it spun and hit the bank and rolled the car at the 29 K marker, causing serious damage to the car, but fortunately not to the driver. Meanwhile, Fritz was taking turns marked "Slow to 20 kph" - which translates to about 12 mph - at around 80 (mph, not kph). He was still running bias ply tires on the Lincoln, which allowed him to drift into the turns, sprint car style.

After passing a few more cars, Fritz came up on the Dodge D-500, which was travelling between 100 and 110 mph. He signaled to pass, but the driver of the Dodge decided to be stubborn and wouldn't let him. Fritz was never one to back down from a challenge, so after they both passed a few other cars, Fritz made his move. The Dodge took a turn on the inside at about 80, so Fritz blew by him on the outside in the Lincoln at about 90. After that, the Dodge seemed to lose some of his motivation, and faded into the distance. Now cruising at around 120, Fritz noticed the stock temperature gauge indicating a bit warm, so he throttled back to about 100. He also noticed the gas gauge was getting a bit low. We had hoped to get better mileage, but such is life at 120 mph.

Fritz began looking forward to the mandatory pit stop. He continued to eat up mile after mile of road, passing whoever he came upon. He came around a curve where a flagman was motioning him to go faster. Wanting to oblige, he increased speed, only to round another corner and find himself right on top of the entrance to the pits. He hit the brakes, flew past the entrance, then burned some good rubber off the tires backing up. After the race, when I asked him about the pit stop, he replied, "Everything went fine until I got out of the car." The racing fuel which had been promised never materialized. And there wasn't any water available either, and the Lincoln needed some, having developed a small crack in the top tank of the radiator. We figured this was probably caused by the roads between Estero Beach and Ensenada, which resembled the impact area at an artillery range. Fortunately, there was a tourist at the pit stop who had been told to pull off the road because of the race, and he gave Fritz a gallon of water out of his camper. Fritz then spent the next six or seven minutes of his ten-minute pit stop frantically looking for anyone with some spare gas. Finally, the support team of the '27 Bugatti said they had ten gallons of Mexican regular that he was welcome to use. He ran up the hill to the Bugatti support vehicle, grabbed two five-gallon cans of gas, and ran back down the hill. Two kind souls dumped the gas into the tank while he poured the water into the radiator. The radiator wasn't full, but it was announced that he had ten seconds to go, so he slammed the hood and made a rather hasty departure from the pits. He arrived at the starting line just in time to get his final three second count down, and he was off.

After he left, the car was running beautifully. The temperature went down and the road straightened out and sloped slightly down hill. By this time he had passed all of the cars in his class and started working on the Porsches, Ferraris, Allards, a couple of Corvettes, and so on. He pushed the throttle down, but the car didn't seem to want to exceed 120. Knowing the Lincoln was good for more than that, he was puzzled for a second until he realized the windows were still down. He put them up and instantly the car's speed increased to 125. It wasn't long, though, before the temperature gauge started to climb again, and he had to slow down to between 100 and 115. Feeling a little warm himself, he decided to put the windows back down.

He told me of a few interesting experiences he had during the race. One thing which caught his attention occurred when a horse almost wandered onto the road in front of him. More interesting yet was when he saw a hay truck with more than a full load coming at him head on. Fortunately, both were able to get more or less in their own lane. Fritz wasn't sure who was more surprised, the truck driver seeing a 4000 plus pound Lincoln drifting around a corner at 100 mph, or himself, seeing a Kenworth tractor with two trailers coming at him on a supposedly closed road.

At last the finish line was in sight. Recalling what had been said at the drivers meeting about crossing the line at high speed if they chose to do so, Fritz pushed the Lincoln back to 120, thinking perhaps they had timing lights set up at the line to catch the cars' speeds. He should have remembered this was the same meeting where they said there would be water and gas, though, because about 200 yards before the finish line a car pulled out in front of him, followed by a couple of spectators wandering across the road, followed by two other cars. Locking up all four wheels, he decided to broad slide to the left for about 50 yards, then to the right for another 50 yards, released the brakes, hit them again, almost slid into the dirt, corrected again, slid to the left again, then to the right again, and ended up in the dirt in front of the timing stand at a 90 degree angle to the road, about six inches from the timing stand barricade. After making a few comments about the lack of security to keep people and vehicles off the roadway at the finish line, he handed the timer his timing slip and was given his receipt.

While he was waiting for me to arrive, Fritz spent

29

some of his time taking photos and talking to the drivers of the other cars as they came across the finish line. We had planned to recreate the finish when I arrived in the chase vehicle so we could record it on film for posterity. However, before I could get there yet another overloaded hay truck came down the road and tore down the finish banner. Such is racing in Mexico.

Fritz also helped some of the other competitors with various mechanical issues. Bill Stroppe had run out of gas just as he came across the finish, so Fritz gave him enough to at least get his car on the trailer. The Thunderbird had overheated and blown a head gasket. Fritz and the owner tried patching it together enough to get it into San Felipe, but it didn't make it very far. We ended up towing the T-bird into San Felipe with the Lincoln using a piece of rope. Granted, people thought it was a bit unusual to tow with a race car, but the reality was that it was far better suited than the Corvair powered VW camper would have been.

That evening the vintage cars entered were supposed to be judged at a car show at the Hotel Castel in San Felipe. While Fritz cleaned, polished, and put even more finishing touches on the Lincoln, I spent over an hour trying to learn where the judging was to be held. After my exercise in futility I retuned to the car, only to learn that there was no official car show after all. It was true there were men at that moment judging some of the cars, however we were told ours had been judged the night before. This was inconvenient, because the previous night the car was filthy. So, the '27 Bugatti won, Fritz was disappointed, but, oh well. I found it easier to take these things more philosophically.

Later that evening was the dinner and awards ceremony. The fastest car in the race was a Porsche RS who had an average speed of 114 over the 120 mile course. The driver attributed this in part to the fact that he lost his brakes near the beginning of the race, and slowing down wasn't really an option. Later I received a revised version of the results in which a '64 Corvette won at a speed of 113.9. The car in our class that came closest to us was the Dodge D-500, who had averaged around 79 mph. We kept listening and waiting, but our number was never called and our time not announced. I was starting to wonder exactly what Fritz had said to the official at the timing stand when he was complaining about the way the finish was handled. Diplomacy was seldom his strong suit when he was annoyed. Ever since Fritz had crossed the finish line, though, people had been congratulating him for doing so well.

After being congratulated so many times, we were a little curious ourselves, so we went in search of the officials, who told us our time had not been recorded on their computer printout of the results. This led us to a search for the official timer, Angus. We wandered from building to building in the hotel complex trying to find some logic to their numbering system. At length we found his room, only to learn that he wasn't there. Discouraged, but not defeated, we decided to return to the party to continue the search when we met him in the hall, along with his assistant time keeper Nolan White. Nolan was a long time SCTA and SDRC (San Diego Roadster Club) member, and undeniably one of the fastest men in the world. Angus assured us that he had indeed computed our time, and even Nolan seemed somewhat impressed. The Lincoln's average speed was 88.11, making us the winner in our class and 20th of the over 100 cars entered. Not bad for a car that I drove to the grocery store on a regular basis. And, we even beat Bill Stroppe, which is something not many people can say.

We spent the next few days relaxing in San Felipe

with the kids, playing in the Sea of Cortez and eating lots of butter clams. All in all, a successful venture, but El Mirage season was approaching, and it was time to get back to work on the Harley for the May meet.

It was in July of 1987 that Fritz decided to ask his six-year-old son Zeke if he should marry me. I'm not quite sure what would have happened if Zeke had said no. I decided that since Fritz had been married twice before, that this wedding should be something different. I wanted to get married at Bonneville during Speed Week, where we had met two years earlier. I contacted the Wendover chamber of commerce and found a very helpful woman who seemed almost as excited about the idea as I was. She put me in contact with the local Presbyterian minister, set up a free room at the State Line Hotel and free dinner at the Peppermill Casino for our wedding night, and put our story in the local paper.

A few weeks earlier, in late June, Fritz was getting the Harley ready to run on the salt. I can't remember why he had it on a trailer going to Long Beach, but I remember vividly that he was going over some railroad tracks and the rope he was using to tie the bike to the trailer came loose, and the bike fell off the trailer on to the tracks. In retrospect, I'm grateful there wasn't a train coming, but the fall did considerable damage. Fortunately, back then there was a motorcycle swap meet in Costa Mesa occasionally, and we were lucky enough to find some of the replacement parts we needed there. Between that and scrounging a few other sources, and Fritz's ability to make anything out of nothing, after a summer of intensive work again to the exclusion of almost everything else - except taking the kids to the beach when it got too hot to work on the Harley - we were able to get the bike both looking and running good once more, just in time for Speed Week.

At this time, there were speed minimums at SCTA/

BNI sanctioned Bonneville events that had to be met to qualify for a record attempt. The minimum in our class was 121 mph. We began the week on Saturday running in the 119 mph range, which was close, just not quite close enough. Our wedding was scheduled for Tuesday, August 25, with the plan being to get married at the starting line. On Monday the heavens opened and the racing surface was flooded. This meant nobody could even go out to the pits on Tuesday, let alone race. Or get married on the starting line. The logical alternative was to get married at "Road's End," - the place where the pavement ends and nothing but salt begins. My sister Sally was my matron of honor, but Fritz was in a bit of a quandary. Two of his best friends were there, Dick and Jim, and he didn't want to offend either of them by asking the other to be his best man. He solved his dilemma by asking Multy Aldrich, a Bonneville racing legend in his own right, who was in charge of hospitality and making sure people had pit passes before they went on to the salt. Every year he and his wife Vera had a box of stuffed animals they would pass out to the kids who were dragged out there by their parents, including mine. Dick had brought a suit for Fritz to wear, thinking he could talk him into it. I told him there wasn't much chance, but he could try. I knew I was right when Fritz told me he would either wear shoes or pants, but not both. I chose the pants option, which I still feel was the right decision.

I changed into my dress in the port-a-potty. It was not a classic long white wedding dress - I'd already been down that road, and it was neither necessary nor appropriate this time. My niece Stacey thought having to change in a port-a-potty was really sad, but one works with what is available. Since nobody could get out on the salt and there were a lot of bored racers that day, my wedding was well attended. I was told afterward that it was shown on ESPN, even went into reruns, although I never saw it. The security guard handcuffed Fritz and I together as a joke until after the ceremony. I later discovered this frightened poor little six-year-old Zeke, who thought his dad and Gayle were going to be hauled away to jail! Dick and Sally had gone to the market in town and bought a sheet cake, which Dick decorated. He and my sister, an excellent photographer, provided me with wedding photos, although my favorite was taken by another friend, Dan, which shows Fritz and me standing in the water beyond the Bonneville sign.

I won't go into the details of our wedding night, although I was grateful to Sally for babysitting so we could spend it alone. We were using the Corvair powered VW bus for our support vehicle, and the next day, Fritz wrote a quotation taken from an old Mad Magazine across the back in black shoe polish. It read: "The Family That Honeymoons Together Eats Prunes Together." One of the people who read it either had too much sun or too much beer, because he reflected, "You know, that's true."

Later that week, as soon as the salt was dry enough, it was back to racing as usual, also known as beating our heads against the wall trying to squeeze that little bit extra out of the bike. Fritz changed jetting, I changed spark plugs, and we changed ignition timing. Neither advancing nor retarding the timing was remotely helpful, so we changed it back before we even attempted a run. Just to clarify, we would make a change, and make a run, make another change, and another run, and so on in an attempt to determine what was working and what wasn't. No matter what we tried, though, the bike was still stuck one mile per hour short of the record, give or take a few tenths. During the course of all these attempts, the gas tank developed a leak at the pet cock, so Fritz decided to braise it. Even though he thoroughly flushed it with water first to eliminate any of the highly combustible fumes, when people saw him preparing to braise the fuel tank they hastily vacated the immediate area. I guess they had all either heard stories of exploding gas tanks or had an unfortunate experience with it. Fritz wasn't concerned though, as he felt confident in his abilities. His real concern was damaging the paint, as Ed 'Big Daddy' Roth had just done the lettering on the tank as a sort of wedding present, but we were too close to give up. Finally, it was the last chance of the week to qualify. The sun was about to sink below the horizon and we were the first of three race vehicles lined up for one last ditch effort.

We decided to put our friend Kevin on the bike, who was an accomplished road racer on the European circuit. As Kevin weighed about 40 pounds less than Fritz, we hoped this would give us the edge we needed. Fritz's famous last words to Kevin as he was about to leave the starting line were, "Don't worry about over-revving it!" and he was off. At about two-thirds track, Kevin thought he was in fourth gear, but unfortunately, he was mistaken. As he wound it out in third, the front cylinder exploded like a hand grenade, leaving pieces of cast iron spread across the salt. It also left the two racers behind us frustrated and disappointed, as it took until after dark to collect all the pieces, using our Frisbee as a container. The good side of this was Kevin's helmet and leathers protected him from all of the shrapnel. The cylinder head was still hanging from the motor mount, with a stretch of twilight between it and the cases, with the connecting rod seeming to just sway in the breeze. After all we had been through with that bike during the course of the summer, I went into the port-a-potty and cried. And yes, that was our honeymoon.

I'm glad he wore pants...

Chapter 5
What's In a Number?

1988 began with the arrival of our son Jason on January 4th. We hadn't actually settled on a name for him yet when I went into labor, so we decided to stop by the library for a book on baby names on the way to the hospital. While I was asking the librarian where the baby name books were, I had a contraction, which really panicked the poor woman. She ran to the shelves, grabbed a couple of books, and had me checked out in no time flat. We drove the '54 Lincoln to the hospital that day, all decked out in its road race regalia. It was definitely easy to spot our car in the parking lot. The delivery room was full, so they had to pull curtains around me in the hall, as Jason didn't want to wait that long to be born. Apparently, we had another racer in the family.

Also during the winter, after dry lakes season had ended, we'd started to prepare for more road racing in the spring in Baja, Mexico. Our friend Fred wanted to take his '48 Packard, so Fritz spent a good deal of time working on it. Unfortunately, due to last minute health problems, Fred was unable to go. So the Lincoln, which still served its primary purpose as everyday transportation, got a quick basic tune up, plugs, points, condenser, and aside from a few adjustments to the suspension and having a slight leak in the radiator repaired, was deemed race ready. Fritz also replaced the stock fan with a steel flex fan to increase horsepower at high speeds. He also chose to remove the belt from the generator and the power steering, running a single belt from the crank pulley to the water pump. The lack of power steering was to aid the cars tracking ability. Another decision Fritz made was to change from bias ply tires to Goodyear Eagle radials. This one he hesitated on, as he really enjoyed the sprint car style slide that the bias plies provided, but thought actually sticking to the road might cut his time from last year.

When it was time to go, we loaded up the Lincoln with our tools, camping gear, etc., grabbed the kids, and headed down to sunny Baja. Our VW camper, last year's support vehicle, had a slight case of "clutchitis", so instead our friends Barry and Sandy took their Dodge van to serve as our support vehicle.

The trip to Ensenada was uneventful, which for one of our trips was nearly miraculous. Once we reached the Estero Beach race headquarters, we checked out some of the competition and proceeded to the registration area. After we took a number, Fritz and I decided to make the most efficient use of our time. I sat with Sandy, sipping complimentary Tecate beer, eating chips and salsa, watching the kids and waiting for our number to be called. Fritz and Barry went to find a tech inspector, which went quite smoothly. The only problem with registration at all was we had been given #52 instead of #54, which was emblazoned on our doors in huge red numbers. This seemed slightly inconvenient, but we covered our existing numbers fairly successfully with the stickers given to us. That detail attended to, Fritz changed the Lincoln's oil and did some bench racing, and his faithful pit crew played on the beach.

There was a drivers' meeting that evening in Ensenada, emphasizing driving safely and not passing in blind corners. The start was also different from the previous year. To accommodate the number of entries, after the 'false start' in downtown Ensenada, there would be a rolling start at the 10 Kilometer marker outside of town, with the cars leaving at 30 second intervals. Fritz was a bit skeptical of how well this would work, but agreed it was worth a try. The rest of the drivers' meeting consisted of the usual mutual admiration society for how well things had gone to this point. I am in no way trying to disparage the people who organized the race - I know a great deal of effort and hard work went into it, and they deserved to pat each other on the back. After the meeting we returned to the Estero Beach campground for a good night's sleep in Barry and Sandy's tent.

The next day we transferred all unnecessary objects from the Lincoln to Barry's van. All that remained in the trunk was the spare tire, the jack, a quart of oil, a gallon of gas, and our trusty can of nitromethane additive. While Fritz was lining up for the false start, Sandy and I passed out some citrus fruit we had brought from home to the local kids. After we ran out of fruit and were preparing to leave town, she and I had a slight problem when we needed to answer the call of nature. Yes, the pit crew had to make a pit stop. Outside the public restroom at the Plaza Civica sat an old man asking for ten *pesos*, which was worth less than a penny at the time, for the use of the facilities. Toilet paper, naturally, was extra. We gave him a quarter for the four of us who needed the *baño*, but after we were finished he wanted more money, which we felt compelled to give him. I guess you could say he got us both coming and going.

Even though a navigator was allowed, Fritz chose to drive the course alone, as he felt he could drive harder that way. Aside from a number of motorcycles, there were 135 car entries, ranging from Alfa Romeos to Z-28s, including the usual exotics - Lotuses, Morgans, a Lancia, an Allard, and so on, along with the customary Ferraris and

Diary of a Racer's Wife

Jags, a whole flock of Porsches, a Dodge D-500, a Willies Jeep (with our number 54) and numerous others, including three 1954 Lincolns, counting ours. Fritz started 114th, which suited him well, as passing other cars was half the fun of road racing.

After waving and honking his way through Ensenada, he reached the "rolling start". I use the term lightly - there was still a bit of a wait before the actual racing started. Fritz started last of the three Lincolns, but had passed the other two within the first few minutes of the race. Fritz soon decided that the radial tires weren't as much fun as the bias plies because he couldn't broad slide sprint car style through the corners anymore. He spent most of the first half of the race passing Porsches, as well as some of the Ferraris, Morgans, Alfa Romeos, the Dodge D-500, etc.

There was one particular stretch where Fritz thought he had dropped a cylinder. He had his foot mashed so hard on the throttle that his leg started to shake, but the speedometer wouldn't climb over 110 mph. He rounded a turn and felt the car being pushed to the right, along with a good deal of desert sand. His temporary loss of power was in reality a headwind, and when it became a cross wind it took about a quarter turn on the steering wheel to compensate for it. Bear in mind, a 1954 Lincoln weighs about 4400 pounds and it takes considerable force to move it sideways. Before long, though, he was past that stretch of road and reached the mandatory ten-minute pit stop.

Meanwhile, Fritz's intrepid pit crew - me, Barry, Sandy, and my sons Andy and Jason - were still trying to find our way out of Ensenada. Our map had several non-existent streets, but that was okay, because the streets that did exist weren't marked anyway. It was to the point that I wasn't sure if things looked familiar because I'd been that way with Fritz in the past or because we were driving around in circles so much.

Returning to the race, the pit stop had been moved from Valle de la Trinidad to Independencia. Fritz had just passed an Alfa Romeo when he saw what he thought were race officials flagging him in. It turned out he was about 400 yards before the real pit stop, and the Alfa passed him. Truth is, that was the only time anyone passed him during the entire race. Fritz quickly figured out what was happening and pulled back on the road, repassed the Alfa, and slid into the real pits. He poured about seven gallons of gas into the tank. We were better prepared this year, as we had learned from experience to have our own gas sent ahead. Fritz checked the water, oil, and tires, then waited and waited until at last they called his number and he was off. Zero to 90 in 22 seconds in a seriously heavy car.

Fritz was flying down the road, passing the ubiquitous Porsche or the occasional Aston Martin. As he passed through Valle de la Trinidad, some of the local kids decided to get their thrills by playing 'dodge car' - running out into the road in front of oncoming race cars. Personally, playing 'chicken' with a 4400 pound car moving at 120 mph isn't my idea of a real good time. After braking to avoid them and thinking a few choice words, it was back to racing as usual.

Back in Ensenada it was getting to the point to where we were thinking, "So what if it's a one- way street? We're only going one way."

For Fritz, the second half of the course was dotted with long straightaways between clusters of mountainous curves. It was on these straightaways that Fritz was able to see what the Lincoln was capable of. It ate mile after mile of Mexican highway at speeds between 125-130 mph. If engines could smile, the Lincoln's little 317 would have been grinning from rocker cover to rocker cover.

41

Diary of a Racer's Wife

Meanwhile, back in Ensenada, I was at last sure that I saw a familiar sight. It was a dip in the road where last year a Mexican entered Mustang had spun out right in front of us. That *would* be the kind of thing I remembered. In any event, that road led us out of Ensenada and to the highway at last.

Fritz was having a great time. There was an accident involving an overturned Porsche, but the occupants were both fine and waved him on. There was one series of mountain curves where Fritz had to slow down briefly. Yet another Porsche was in front of him running at about 80 mph and Fritz couldn't see far enough to pass. As I've mentioned before, just because something is supposed to be a 'closed course' in Mexico doesn't mean the occasional farmer won't pull onto the main highway from a dirt road in his truck or that the occasional burro won't wander onto the road. Not wanting to push the driver of the Porsche beyond his capabilities, Fritz decided to bide his time until they were out of the turns and he was able to pass safely.

Near the end of the race, Fritz came to what appeared to be a gradual turn, driving into it at about 110. He realized the turn was starting to tighten up on him, but he was already committed and there was no slowing down at that point. He envisioned the car getting into the 'marbles' at the edge of the road and sliding off into the desert. He told me it was a helpless feeling - if you accelerate, you fly off the road; if you back off, you spin out first and then fly off the road. All he could do was massage the throttle pedal a little and hang on. When we were discussing this after the race, I asked him if he saw his life flash before his eyes. He said no, he was too distracted by the XKE Jaguar stuck upside down on the side of the cliff. Apparently, that driver had an experience similar to Fritz's, but he hadn't been as fortunate and had spun out of control. When we passed by later in the van, we saw the mangled scrap metal that used to be a piece of precision machinery. Amazingly, considering the condition of the wreckage, the driver walked away. It wasn't long after that tricky turn that the finish line was in sight. Fritz sailed over the line at around 100 mph, with cars and spectators within six inches of either side of him. Not exactly the safest situation in the world, but, as I've said innumerable times, such is racing in Mexico.

After turning in his timing slip, he spent the next couple of hours watching the remainder of the racers cross the finish line, talking with other drivers, accommodating people who wanted their photo taken with the Lincoln, etc. One man asked if he could have a photo taken sitting inside the car, so Fritz, in his usual style, handed him a helmet and said, "Sure, take it for a spin if you want." As time passed, my husband started to wonder what had become of his family and friends, aka pit crew. He was considering driving back toward Ensenada to look for us when the driver of the Dodge D-500's support vehicle approached him. The transmission in his one-ton Ford had catastrophically failed (in other words, he fried it) and he was looking for someone to tow him into San Felipe. Having nothing better to do at the time, Fritz volunteered to help.

He told Jack, the driver, to wait where he was, and came back in the Lincoln to take him the 20 miles or so to his broken-down van. Jack looked at him and protested, "But this is a race car! You can't tow a one-ton van with a race car, can you?" After Fritz assured him the Lincoln was capable of towing anything up to and including a Mack truck, Jack gratefully accepted and climbed in. They had progressed about ten miles out of town when they had to pull over to add a little gas to the Lincoln and answer the call of nature.

It was then that his wayward pit crew came on the scene. After the usual hugs and kisses, the boys and I hopped into the Lincoln with Fritz and proceeded to take Jack to his van. The only problem we encountered was with Jack's lack of experience being towed with a cable. I suppose it's an art form that I learned to take for granted, as Fritz and I had many occasions over the years to perfect it. It wasn't long, however, before we had safely returned to San Felipe, although somehow we had gotten separated from Barry and Sandy during the towing process. They were bringing up the rear in their van, and we couldn't see them behind the van we were towing. We delivered Jack to race headquarters and briefly surveyed the situation there before returning to town to search for our pit crew. Luck was with us, and we found them without much difficulty. This meant we weren't at the hotel for the official concourse judging. It didn't make much difference to us though. Last year we had scrubbed and polished, all to no avail. This year we simply had no time for that sort of thing.

We returned to the hotel for dinner and the awards ceremony. While we were waiting, Fritz chatted with some of the other drivers. The driver of another '54 Lincoln told Fritz there was no way he could keep up with him in the turns, blaming it in part on his brakes fading. Fritz looked at him innocently and said, "Brakes? Gee, I don't use mine."

Dinner was quite good. We sat with the D-500 crew, and Jack couldn't do enough for us. He stood in line to get dinner for Andy and me. He would have returned to get some for Fritz as well, but Fritz was already in line taking care of that. They began by serving steak, chicken and shrimp, but after that ran out served more standard Mexican fare, such as enchiladas and chili rellenos. It was all delicious.

After dinner the various awards were given out, including the concourse awards. I find it necessary to digress here for a moment. Following last year's La Carrera, Fritz and I spent a few extra days in San Felipe. In the space of two days I managed to eat 189 steamed butter clams - 94 one day and 95 the next. It was also about that time that our son Jason was conceived. It became a running joke between Fritz and me that the clams were the cause of this. At this year's race, Fritz happened to mention this story to a couple of gentlemen who, unknown to him, were the concourse judges.

As the other awards were being given out, I noticed two men standing in front of me going over what I assumed to be a list of some of the awards. My ears perked up when I overheard one of them ask the race coordinator who Fritz Kott was. The coordinator replied, "You know. The one with the baby."

The judges looked at each other and said, "Oh, Jason's father." Jason was the hit of the evening - a real party animal before he was old enough to walk.

When it was time for the concourse awards, the judges began by speaking briefly about the third place winner, a '53 Porsche. They then began to tell *my* clam story to approximately 200 people at the ceremony, and asked Fritz, Jason and I to come up and accept the second place award. I wasn't sure whether I was more shocked at winning second place in the concourse with a dirty car that hadn't even been present at the judging, or embarrassed at having my rather voracious appetite for clams and the ensuing consequences announced to the world.

After the other awards were given, it was time for the awards we really cared about, speed. We knew Fritz had done well, but when our class was announced we were not mentioned. We had been through this the year before, and it was quite frustrating. It was almost enough to give me a perseccution complex.

We approached the race chairman and told him that we had once more been ignored. He referred us to the Long Beach MG Club, which was in charge of the timing this year, and gave us the appropriate room number. After locating the timer's room, we were told to return at ten a.m. the next day. This was disappointing, but we didn't have much choice.

We camped that night at the campground next door to the hotel. While driving there at around eleven p.m. it suddenly got very dark. Fritz and I looked at each other perplexed until the realization hit us - we hadn't taken the duct tape safety mask off of the headlights, and had just left the lighted area of the hotel. In our defense, it had been a long day.

The next morning, we were told they had computed our time. It seemed when Fritz crossed the finish line the officials couldn't decide if he was #52 or #54, so they didn't bother with him the night before. The large stick-on #52 they had given us at tech covered most of the permanent #54, but apparently there was still room for confusion. We eagerly went to look at the revised time sheet, only to discover we had been given an average speed of 89.98, which was only slightly better than the year before. That may not sound bad, but we knew it wasn't right. The Lincoln didn't have any cooling problems this year and there were no wrecks to slow him down. It was very disappointing, to say the least.

It wasn't until after we had returned home and done a little detective work that we determined our true average speed. What had happened was this: for some inexplicable reason, Fritz had been kept in the pits a full four minutes too long. When the timers deducted the ten-minute pit stop from his total time, they didn't notice the extra four minutes, which obviously led to a much lower average. When Fritz entered the pits, the time was written on a tag on the side of the car. When he left the pits, he happened to have the tape recorder on as he was being sent out, and recorded the official stating the actual time. After we worked that out, it was a simple matter to recalculate. Fritz had maintained an average speed of 102.24, and thereby won the historic class instead of taking third. It also moved him up in the overall standings from 38th to 11th out of 135 total entries.

Getting this officially changed though, proved to be more of a challenge than it was worth, and we eventually chose to let the matter drop. Besides, Fritz knew what he and the car were capable of, and figured if he could do it once, he could do it again.

Summer arrived, and with it a new project. Fritz began building a flathead V8 for a '50 Mercury, which an acquaintance would run in the La Carrera Panamericana, more commonly known as the Mexican Road Race. This race would be held in the fall, and would extend the length of Mexico, from Tuxtla Gutierrez near the Guatemalan border up to Juarez, on the Texas border. Fritz wanted to test the engine he had built for the Merc, and decided that Bonneville would be an excellent proving ground, so he put it in our Model A roadster pickup, and off we went. Okay, getting ready for Speed Week wasn't quite that easy. For one thing, there were different criteria for loading when taking the motorcycle. I got so I could do that in my sleep,which is good, because I sometimes had to. But, after a week or two of feverish activity, including finding places to put a couple hundred gallons of Pick-A-Part gas, and the occasional temper tantrum by an aggravated racer, we were on our way.

At this point I think I should clarify that when we went to Bonneville, we didn't have a nice fancy trailer with everything all contained inside like sensible people.

Diary of a Racer's Wife

We had, at this point, a '72 Ford station wagon with gear piled in and on it, and a borrowed tent courtesy of Barry and Sandy. We set up the tent at the gravel pits, and I remember one evening the wind was howling so much that I had to stay sitting up for most of the night holding the main support pole upright so the whole thing wouldn't collapse on my tired, sleeping family. By about four a.m., the wind abated enough that I could give up my silent and uncomfortable vigil, and fall asleep for a few hours. I seem to recall the tent still fell on us to some degree, but at least I was no longer worried about anyone suffocating under it.

Tech inspection was not a particular problem this year, so soon we had established our pit and begun the process of waiting in line, making a run, getting a time, checking the engine, and repeating the procedure. It is required that you use the 'event gasoline' when trying to qualify for a record during Speed Week. Fritz was more interested in seeing how the engine would run on pump gas, though, as that would be closer to what was available in Mexico.

We had made a couple of runs when we developed a major problem with the engine. The combustion chambers had blown out of a couple of cylinders in the brand new Edelbrock heads. Fritz was somewhat annoyed by this, but undaunted. When he was racing, what could be considered a catastrophic failure to some was relegated to the category of an inconvenience to him. It was too early in the week to give up and go home, so we drove into Wendover in search of an old unused '49 to '53 Ford car with its engine intact. We were able to find a '53 Ford coupe in someone's back yard, so all we had to do was find the owner and ask if we could borrow his cylinder heads for the week, with the promise of reinstalling them at the end of the week. Fritz managed to convince this guy, a total stranger, of his intentions and honesty, and he agreed to let us borrow his heads. Like I said before, when he was motivated, he had a real way with people.

The next day we were running again. The compression ratio was a bit different, but the engine ran well. While we didn't set any records - in reality since we were running pump gas we weren't trying to - the runs we made during the week were definitely a successful test for the engine before the Panamericana. And, true to Fritz's word, when we were done with the heads we returned them and reinstalled them on the '53 Ford from whence they came. We did talk to Edelbrock after the meet to get them to replace the cylinder heads, as the combustion chambers must have had some porosities when they were cast. At first the owner was reluctant, blaming the event gas of that year, as other people had experienced similar problems with different vehicles. Once Fritz explained that we had been using pump gas because of the nature of our testing, and not the event gas, they finally agreed to stand behind their product and replace the heads. Good news, considering our upcoming plans for the engine.

The Original Full House Mouse

Chapter 6

Pan Am-demonium

When I originally wrote the article about this race for the Road Race Lincoln Register, I compared it to Homer's "Odyssey." Reflecting back, I stand behind that analogy. I mean, throw in a hydra, and we were there! Although thinking about it, the sirens we heard weren't beautiful women sitting on rocks, they were coming from the cars of the *Federales*. During the summer, we had heard the organizers of the La Carrera Classic were going to resurrect the much longer La Carrera Panamericana. Naturally, we were all for it, with the minor problem of coming up with the $2500 entry fee. Fritz and I went to visit Tom, owner of the Ontario Pick-A-Part, our gas sponsor, and all around good guy. And yes, I would still say that even if he hadn't agreed to provide the entry fee for the race. Tom was willing, the company name was already on the car, and we officially entered the Pan Am.

Coming up with the funding for the entry turned out to be the easy part, though. Fritz not only had the Lincoln to prepare, but was involved in building the '50 Mercury for fellow competitor Dan S. The engine had proven itself at Bonneville, but the rest of the car was another story. This car had been used by Sylvester Stallone in the movie "Cobra", and when the filming was over, it looked like the loser in a demolition derby. Dan had hired a custom body shop in the San Fernando Valley to do the body work, glass, suspension, wiring, etc. Dan's plan was to have the car finished in time to be shipped on the transport that was taking other race cars down to Tuxtla Gutierrez on the Guatemalan border for the start of the race. Our plan was to drive the Lincoln down the Baja California Peninsula to Cabo San Lucas, take the ferry across to Puerto Vallarta, drive through Acapulco down the coast, then heading inland to Tuxtla. The best laid plans of mice and men ... and racers.

Work on the Mercury was taking longer than expected, so naturally Fritz decided to go up to the Valley, about 150 miles north, and help them out. What he assured me would be "just a day or two" turned into three weeks, night and day, with him getting home around four or five in the morning, when he came home at all. I told him he was lucky to have such an understanding wife.

Our plan had been to leave on our 2600 mile journey into Mexico on Friday, October 21, which would give us plenty of time for a leisurely drive. Friday came, and the Lincoln still sat on jack stands in the front yard, its suspension lying in front of it in pieces. Fritz had to make one last 300 mile round trip to the Valley to help with the Mercury, which had, during the process of its assembly, been given the dubious title of "Copacabana." Since the Copacabana had missed its shipping date, the revised plan was for everyone to meet at our house Saturday in the hopes that we would be able to leave together Sunday. Missing the shipping date turned out to be a blessing in disguise - the car transport that was carrying about eight race cars had overturned near Guadalajara. Two of the cars, a Porsche and a Lincoln, were completely totaled. The rest sustained varying degrees of damage. A team of American mechanics was sent down to repair as many of the cars as possible.

Saturday, our ranch was a frenzy of activity. Barry and Sandy came over to help get the front suspension together on the Lincoln. Tim E., who was going with us as support crew, was there preparing his El Camino for the journey. While work was progressing steadily on the Lincoln, Fritz kept finding things to do to it - while repairing the suspension, he noticed the front motor mounts were completely worn out, so not having time to find original equipment replacements, he fabricated a pair out of some Dodge truck transmission mounts picked up from a friend. Fritz then decided he needed to braise up a couple of thin spots in the oil pan and straighten it, and in the process noticed the timing chain was loose.

Around 1:30 a.m., Tim's brother, Jim, who was also to go with us, showed up with the Mercury. Sometime after daybreak our friend Greg showed up with a timing chain. Fritz already had new sprockets, but the chain he had ordered never materialized. Before we could leave he still had to mount and plumb a 30 gallon fuel tank in the trunk, making a firewall for it from aluminum and fire retardant fiberglass, and figure out how to hook up a twelve volt CB radio in a car with a six volt battery. He ended up making an aluminum battery box and mounting a twelve volt battery on the floor in the back seat. He wanted to mount a siren on the car, but decided instead to rig up a handle for an old siren we had lying around, powered by the same battery as the CB, which would be my responsibility to use. It was a bit heavy and awkward, but turned out to be very effective.

Since much of the race was being run as a rally, we had looked into getting a proper rally computer. But, since time was short and money was even shorter, we decided to use our back up computer - me. I would use a stopwatch and a calculator, and a '34 Ford speedometer with the face laid out in one mile per hour increments up to 90. We still had our old standby 160 mph Stewart Warner speedometer, too.

Somewhere during all of this and trying to find spare rims, change tires, and so on, Sunday blended into Monday and good friend Jim T. came out to help, bringing us another left exhaust manifold for the Lincoln. Monday blended into early Tuesday. Fritz had slept two hours Sunday night, and not at all on Monday night. I was the lucky one - I got about three hours each night. Jim E. returned with his friend Cathy, comprising the rest of the pit crew, arriving at the ranch Tuesday about 2 a.m. At 3 a.m. Fritz had gasoline dripping off his elbows installing fuel lines and a three-way valve for the additional gas tank/fuel cell. At 4 a.m., my husband woke me up so I could start loading the car. Finally, 7 a.m. Tuesday, we were ready to leave. Dan would be driving his Mercury, Tim was in his El Camino, Jim and Cathy were in Jim's van, and Fritz, Andy, Jason and I were in the Lincoln. At long last, we headed toward the border.

Our plan was to drive straight through, stopping only for gas and food. It seemed like a good idea at the time. We were heading down Interstate 8 toward Mexicali. We had rearranged drivers - I was driving the Lincoln and Fritz was checking out the Copacabana. While we had run the Mercury's engine in our Model A roadster pickup at Bonneville and at the September El Mirage meet, the whole car as a unit was unproven. About 70 miles from home, Fritz smelled rubber burning, so we all pulled off the freeway to check out the problem. Three of the ribs on the blower belt had disintegrated. Fritz had told someone else to set the tensioner, and in his sleep deprived state had forgotten to double check it himself. We had an extra belt with us, but since seven ribs remained, he decided to loosen it to the proper tension and save the other belt for future usage.

Once again, we headed down the road. We stopped at a gas station in El Centro to try to get directions to a welding shop. We wanted to get tow bar mounts welded to the Merc so we could tow it to save wear and tear on the car. Fritz had planned on doing it himself, but obviously just flat ran out of time. While we were talking to the station attendant, a lady in a Pinto that had been parked next to us backed out and hit the right rear quarter panel of the Lincoln, flattening the stainless trim and taking some of the car's yellow paint with her. She didn't bother to mention it to us, and drove away. Later, when we noticed, we took it in stride. We were too tired to do anything else anyway. Unfortunately, it proved to be a mere foreshadow of what was to come.

We located the welding shop, spent the next couple of hours there, then finally drove the last dozen or so miles to the Mexican border, reaching it at about 4:30 p.m. Mexico at last! Now we only had another 2400 plus miles to go in two days. Piece of cake, right? Once in Mexico we drove parallel to the U.S. border. It looked like we were finally going to start making some time. Somewhere in the desert on the other side of San Luis, Tim, driving his El Camino, smelled gear oil. Concerned that perhaps he had blown a seal in his rear end, we all pulled off the road. Instead of finding a simple problem like losing a pinion seal, or an axle bearing, Tim discovered, much to his horror, that a gallon of 90 weight gear oil had ruptured in the back of the truck, saturating everything with the foul smelling lubricant. If you've never had that experience, consider yourself fortunate. If you have, I feel your pain - it's nasty.

After spending an hour or so dealing with that mess, we were off again toward Sonoita, which is just across the border from Lukeville, Arizona. Once we reached Sonoita, we had another issue to deal with. We had gone about 20 kilometers (12 miles) out of town when we came to a border checkpoint, and were told we could not proceed further without visas. Fritz and I knew this would be occurring at some point, so while it was time consuming and an inconvenience, it wasn't really a problem. At the time, all that was required to get a visa was a birth certificate. Jim and Cathy, however, didn't have their birth certificates with them, but the official was willing to overlook that for an extra $5 each. By this time, Jim and Cathy were no longer enthusiastic about the trip - it had taken 17 hours to go 300 miles - and the U.S. border was looking pretty good to them. They gave us our luggage, tools, and spare parts which they had in the van, and headed back. This presented a bit of a problem for us, as Cathy was supposed to babysit during the race, and we now had a good deal of extra weight in the trunk of the Lincoln, and could no longer "travel light" while racing. But, there was nothing to be done about it.

We returned to the checkpoint without them, where we faced yet another obstacle. Between the three remaining vehicles, we practically had enough spare parts to build another car from the ground up. The official wanted to empty all three vehicles and charge us somewhere around $3000 for "importing new parts" into Mexico. After some three hours of negotiation by Dan, who was from Argentina and spoke fluent Spanish, and a $50 *mordida* (bribe) we were once more on our way. It was by this point 3 a.m., so we drove a little further and pulled over to rest for a couple of hours. Tim, the kids and I got a couple of hours sleep, while Fritz worked on the Mercury, changing the oil, adjusting the points, etc. He took the 12 volt drop light into the back of the El Camino to look for some parts. A short time later, Dan heard a strange noise coming from the back of Tim's truck, and went over to investigate. He found Fritz snoring, face down, drop light in one hand, the other hand reaching for a part. As the sun rose over the cactus dotted desert, we all began trying to wake up cnough to continue our quest. Dan had started applying computerized stick-on lettering and decals to his car at first light. Fritz helped him finish the job, and we prepared to leave.

At this point, Dan decided he could make better time on his own, so he blasted off down the road. His plan was to average around 100 mph, and make it to Tuxtla in a day and a half. Tim, Fritz, the kids and I loaded the two remaining vehicle in our diminishing entourage and headed into the next town, Caborca, to make a phone call. We were seriously considering giving up and going home. We still had 2100 miles to go and a day and a half to get there. Fritz called the U.S. race coordinator's home to find out the logistics of joining the race a day late. We were told that the race had been postponed a day since many other racers were having issues with the border, etc. Our hopes rekindled, we decided to press on. Dan, meanwhile, had hit a railroad crossing at over 100 mph and had gone airborne. While flying through the air he reconsidered his decision to try to average 100 mph all the way to Tuxtla, and decided to rejoin our caravan.

Shortly after meeting up with Dan again, smoke started billowing out from the floorboard on the passenger side of the Lincoln where I was sitting feeding Jason. Fritz made a rather hasty stop, sliding the car sideways off the highway onto a small graveled area. He proceeded to throw everything out of the front seat, including me and the baby, as apparently I wasn't quite quick enough for him on my own. Actually, we were more dragged than thrown. After he had poured some of our drinking water onto the smoldering carpet, we discovered the cause of the smoke. When he had installed the new motor mounts it raised the car's engine enough to cause our modified exhaust to come in contact with the floorboards. Oops. We borrowed a fireproof floor mat from Dan and sandwiched it between the floorboard and the stock mat, at least temporarily alleviating that problem.

Our revised plan was to cut across the top of Mexico, through Agua Prieta, and then over to the Pan American highway. Somehow in Santa Ana we managed to miss our turn, which I personally think never existed, and headed south along the coast instead of east. As we had all basically lost all sense of direction, along with our minds, no one realized we were headed the wrong way until I saw a sign that read, "Hermosillo, 80 Kilometers." This was actually the route Fritz and I had planned on taking after it became impractical to go down Baja California and cross on the ferry, and before we decided to cut across. After a brief conference we decided we would lose more time backtracking than continuing our present course, so we carried on, reaching Guaymas around 5 p.m. Tim had been towing the Merc for a short time with his El Camino when the Copacabana picked up a nail in the right front tire on the outskirts of town. Leaving Tim, Dan and Andy with the other two cars, Fritz, Jason and I took the tire back into Guaymas in the Lincoln to have it repaired. The young man at the tire shop did an excellent job of repairing and remounting the tire. The job was completed in about 15 minutes and cost 3,400 *pesos* (about $1.50). We returned to the rest of our little troop, reinstalled the wheel on the car, and headed on down toward Cuidad Obregon, Los Mochis, and then Culican.

We reached Culican around 5 a.m. and decided to get a hotel room so we could get a couple of hours of sleep. The water in the shower was tepid at best, and nonexistent at worst. A real drag when you've just covered your body with soap. And there wasn't a toilet seat, but there was a bed, the roaches didn't take up too much space on it, and it was nice to be able to stretch out a bit. The Lincoln is a comfortable car, but the front seat really doesn't sleep three well, even when one is just a baby. All too soon it was time to press on.

The terrain had been gradually changing from desert to tropical jungle. Shortly after we crossed the Tropic of Cancer, at least according to the map, Tim had a hair raising experience. He met an oncoming bus about the size of a Greyhound. As the bus drifted around the corner at about 70 mph, it swayed into Tim's lane, leaving a little of its paint on his door handle. That particular stretch of road was heavily strewn with wrecked trucks and buses, some of which had obviously burned to the ground. It was also heavily adorned with shrines and crosses marking the spots at which people's loved ones had lost their lives. Tim nicknamed that stretch of road "Bloody Gulch."

Other than losing Dan briefly in Mazatlan, the rest of the day passed without incident. Shortly after dusk fell, however, Tim, who had mostly recovered from the morning's experience, was in for another.

I need to digress here for a moment to explain about Mexican trucks in that era, for those of you who aren't familiar with them. First, every one we saw was heavily overloaded. Second, they didn't seem to believe in mufflers, although Fritz actually enjoyed the sound. Third, most of them had armor plating and reinforced cattle guards, as well as steel spikes protruding from the lug nuts. If you've ever seen the chariot races in the movie "Ben Hur", it was a lot like that. Finally, and perhaps most importantly to this narrative, they seemed to get their thrills by passing on blind curves, especially while going uphill. Now, back to the story.

We had pulled the Lincoln over to help Dan, who was having a problem with the Merc. In the growing darkness, Tim, who was a few cars behind us, didn't see us pull off the road until he was right next to us, so he continued up the hill to find a place to turn around. As he was coming back toward us, he met two big diesel trucks coming head on, with one in each lane. As neither truck driver was willing to budge an inch, Tim had no choice but to spin out in some poor villager's front yard and watch the trucks, and his life, pass in front of him. When he finally made it back to us he told us he had a weak heart and almost getting killed twice in one day wasn't helping it a bit. After he calmed down a minute we were off toward Guadalajara.

Once we reached Guadalajara, Tim was in need of some gasoline. Fritz and I spotted a station on the other side of the median, signaled for Tim and Dan to turn around, and went back to the station to wait for them. The El Camino pulled in behind us, but the Copacabana drove past us and kept going. Being unable to raise Dan on the CB, Tim went ahead and got gas, then we wandered around the city for a while looking for the Mercury. We had just about given up, and were considering getting a couple of hours of sleep, when we thought we heard Dan's air horn. Temporarily rejuvenated, we took off on another wild goose chase. After wandering around another 30 minutes or so, we decided to go ahead and head down the road to Mexico City.

We had just left a poorly lit side street for the main highway when Fritz suddenly exclaimed, "Oh, no!" and pulled over. There, sitting in the ditch between the highway and the side street, was the Mercury. Fritz ran over to see what had happened while I stayed in the car with the kids.

I saw Dan run toward him, saying, "I'm all right! I'm all right!" Fritz didn't know whether to hug him or slug him, but chose the former option. The car, however, did not fare as well as Dan had. The front fenders now sat at an awkward angle, the headlights were smashed, the hood was askew and the grille looked more like a pile

Diary of a Racer's Wife

of spaghetti than a '50 Merc grille. The right front tire
was parted from its rim, you could tell the suspension
was tweaked, and a pool of coolant sat under the radiator.
About the only other thing you could see in the darkness
was the concrete wall a few feet in front of the car, which
by the grace of God he didn't hit. It was obvious, though,
that the Copacabana wasn't going anywhere under its
own power without some serious work.

Tim took one look at it burrowed into the dirt and
said, "This isn't the Copacabana, it's the Gopher Cabana."
Dan's command of the language once again helped him
out. The *Federales* wanted to impound the car, quite possibly never to be seen again, but some fast talking allowed
us to get a tow truck to pull it out of the soft dirt, which
along with his safety harness, had undoubtedly saved
Dan's life. He told us he had been traveling at over 100
mph when the side street he was on came to an abrupt
end and the car hurtled into the ditch. Once the car was
extricated, we had it towed to a parking lot near the Hotel
Los Reyes where we could work on it in the morning.

We got a couple of rooms and fell into an exhausted sleep at about 4:30 am. We slept longer than three
hours for the first time in many days, getting up around
9:30. Fritz and Tim went over to the parking lot to survey
the damage in the cold light of day, while Dan went to
telephone his fiancé Elisa, who had flown down to Tuxtla to meet him for the start of the race. While he was
on the phone with her, he learned that the race had left
on schedule after all. Meanwhile, Fritz and Tim came
back to give us the verdict on the Gopher Cabana - the
radiator had to be repaired, the steering box had to be
replaced, and some of the suspension components were
damaged, but most of the damage was cosmetic. So, Fritz,
along with our seven-year-old son Andy and Tim, grabbed
sledge hammers and tire irons and pounded the fenders,

hood, grille and splash pan more or less back into shape. They also revamped some of the wiring and straightened the suspension as much as possible with the tools on hand. After accomplishing that, they located a Camaro power steering box and had the radiator repaired.

We spent another night in Guadalajara. By 1:30 Saturday afternoon Fritz and Tim had the Mercury drivable again. We had already missed the first two stages of the race, but were determined not to miss any more. Traffic out of Guadalajara was heavy and slow moving but eventually we made it to Queretaro. On the way there we saw a recent ugly accident, which was very sobering. It was all too obvious there was literally nothing we could do, so we continued on, hearing the sirens of the *Federales* approaching to deal with the carnage.

Around midnight we reached Mexico City, following the signs that marked the way to Puebla, until they ceased to exist. We ended up downtown, lost again. We stopped at a taco stand for some tacos made of left over pig parts - you know, the kind you don't discuss in polite society. I didn't realize this until after I'd eaten one, but, whatever. During the process of buying and eating tacos, Dan got directions, with Fritz catching the word *"aeropuerto"* or airport. Soon after leaving the taco stand and starting back the opposite direction of a parallel one-way street, one of the ones with eight lanes - I'm sure you've seen them in horror movies - Tim pulled over to the right and stopped in a no parking zone. Naturally, we pulled in right behind him. Dan, the only one who knew where we were going, kept right on going out of sight and C.B. range. Tim had pulled over because his lights had malfunctioned. We repaired his problem, and headed off in the direction we had last seen Dan. Since we couldn't find him, but we could find signs for the airport, we decided to go to there and ask directions. We needed gas, so we stopped at the airport Pemex station. Fritz asked a cabbie (*taxista*) the way to Puebla in broken Spanish. He not only gave us directions that we more or less understood, but offered to show us the way to the right road. What a nice guy! We followed him to the highway, tipped him a couple thousand *pesos*, and thought we were on our way at last.

We noticed blue flashing lights in the traffic behind us, but didn't think much of it until Tim's El Camino shot up next us, with Tim yelling, "Hey Fritz, I think these guys want to talk to me!" He was referring to the police car he had left in the dust in his efforts to get to us. His El Camino was not exactly factory issue any more, and didn't have a problem catching us. We all pulled over to wait for the *Federales*. Fritz went back to help Tim, who spoke virtually no Spanish. The police just poked around a little bit and then let us go. We never did figure out why they stopped him. Could it be that we were finally going to make it to the race?

We got into Puebla around 2 a.m. We had no idea where race headquarters was, but guessed it had to be in one of the larger hotels. We asked some people at an all-night restaurant for suggestions. They told us our best bet was to go down 9th Avenue *Sur* (south). After following their directions, we ended up in a rather seedy part of town with no hotels in sight. Thinking perhaps we had misunderstood, since our Spanish wasn't exactly flawless, we tried again, getting similar directions and similar results. This went on for about two and a half hours until we decided to hire another *taxista* to take us to all the hotels until we found the right one. Fortunately, *señor taxista* knew exactly where he was going and took us to the opposite end of the city to the Hotel Mission de Puebla. We happily tipped him and went inside. When we went to check in, however, we were not on the hotel's list, and it took another half hour or so to straighten it out. We did notice Dan's name on their register, so he had made it. Around 5:15 we got the car 'put to bed' in the impound area and headed off for a couple hours sleep.

There was a mandatory drivers' meeting at 9:00 a.m. When we saw Dan looking fresh and rested, he told us that the night before he had pulled over to wait for us, but saw a Panamerican Road Race official's car drive past, so he decided to follow him to the race headquarters. Granted, we were a bit peeved at being abandoned in the middle of the night in one of the largest cities in the world, but we chose to get over it. The poor officials weren't entirely sure what to do with us when we told them our babysitter had abandoned us in Sonoita and that the kids were going to be riding with us. Let's face it, they hadn't anticipated that one when formulating their rule book. But they were our kids and it was our decision, and we had helmets and seat belts for them, so they just washed their hands of the matter.

After the meeting we got our numbers, decals, etc. for the car and went to the impound area to prepare for the day's event. While Fritz was working on the Lincoln, a member of another crew gave me some oil filters and transmission fluid for the car. He told me they had been shipped down for a Lincoln that had been totaled in the transport accident earlier. After doing the required maintenance to the car, we decided we had better get some gas. A Pemex truck was across the street from the hotel for the racers' convenience. We went over to get in line and were motioned to go around. We were then motioned by a policeman to turn left at the corner, and then left again, and then another told us to go straight. We realized this was not the way to the gas line, but were trapped in the flow of traffic and unable to return to the hotel at this point. Well, after about ten blocks of this we turned anyway, backtracking and eventually getting back to get fuel. After accomplishing that, we took off for the starting line, once more following police directions. We kept going in the direction they were pointing, but soon ran out of police with no other race cars in sight. Lost again, and with our starting time only minutes away. I had a route book describing the route to Mexico City from the starting line, but no route to the starting line. While we never did find the starting line, we did eventually find ourselves on one of the streets in the route book, so decided to press on from there. I wondered if we had left Puebla and entered the Twilight Zone. There were cheering crowds, so we figured we must be on the right track. We were actually in the La Carrera Panamericana at last!

The race was laid out as a timed rally with special sections each day for high speed runs. The route that day took us through winding forested mountain roads and small villages. My job as navigator was not only to tell Fritz where to go - I'd had some experience with that as his wife - but also to calculate how fast we had to go to get there at the required time interval. I also had to notify him of towns, turns, and obstacles coming up. Shortly after we left Puebla, we saw the Copacabana off to the side of the road, with Tim also there, changing a tire. We learned later it was the second one they had blown in the first ten kilometers of the race. Since everything seemed to be under control, we continued on course.

We passed through small villages where time seemed to have stopped 100 years ago, including the use of horse drawn wagons for transportation. Every town seemed to have declared a holiday as people lined the streets, waving, cheering and throwing flowers on the pavement in front of us. We began to relax a bit. I had figured out how to read the route book, the kids were be-having, and we were a little ahead of schedule. Our only complaint was that we had worn out our shock bushings on the mountain roads before we ever got to the race, and this was causing a slight vibration in the front end.

Since we were near where the route book said the finish line was and had about 20 minutes to kill, we decided to use the time to look for a set of rubber shock bushings. We checked a couple of places, but were unable to acquire any, so we decided it was time to cross the finish line. The route book said, "Right turn in signal. Dangerous intersection. Caution. Straight. Railroad crossing." We were then supposed to be at the day's final check point. There was only one problem with that. Neither the right turn nor the railroad tracks existed. We turned right at every intersection within a three mile radius of where the book said we should be. We spent an hour frantically looking for the finish line, or at least another racer, but to no avail. We were trying to figure out what to do next when a family in a black sedan pulled up next to us at a traffic light. The driver asked, "Are you lost?" When we replied in the affirmative, he graciously told us to follow him to the impound area. I seriously doubt that we ever would have found it without him. Mexico City makes Los Angeles look like a small town.

The race cars were on display in the parking lot of the Auditorio Nacional, directly across the street from the Hotel Presidente. It was nice to have an opportunity to see some of the competition, which included five other Lincolns. There was also the usual assortment of Porsches, Jags, Fords, Mercurys, Corvettes, Hudsons, etc. I must admit it was the first time I had seen a Czechoslovakian Tatra, however. After looking around a bit, we returned to our Lincoln. I sat in the car with the kids, signing autographs and letting 10-month-old Jason stand in front of the steering wheel and 'drive'. Jason was a hit with all the local women *(Que precioso, que bonito!)* and his photo ended up in one of the Mexico City newspapers the next day, with the caption: "The Happiest Baby in Mexico." Fritz, in addition to signing autographs, had located some shocks for the car from one of the other Lincoln racers, who happened to be the owner of Carrera Shocks. We couldn't really afford the $100, but we couldn't afford not to have the shocks worse, so Fritz went ahead and made the deal. We chose not to go across town to that evening's awards dinner. We really didn't have time, and I was tired of getting lost in Mexico City. So, after eating dinner in one of the hotel's restaurants, Fritz and Tim went to work on the Lincoln, replacing the shocks, then checked Dan's Merc, while the kids and I went to our room on the 22nd floor. What a spectacular view of the city! The view was lovely, but all I really wanted to see was the inside of my eyelids. Poor Fritz and Tim tried to wake me at 2 a.m. to let them in, but I was sleeping too soundly and didn't hear them, and they ended up going down to the desk for another key.

Racing was scheduled to begin at 7:00 in the morning. The start of this day's leg was right across the street in front of the *Auditorio Nacional*. We didn't have to worry about getting lost trying to find it, but we did have to go the wrong way up a one-way street to get there. We had even gotten gas the night before, so it looked like nothing could stop us!

By this point, there were only 69 of the original 125 plus entries still in the race. We were started 68th, due largely to not finding the official start on the previous day. But this was a new day, and we were finally where we needed to be.

Almost immediately after we left the starting line I could tell it was going to be another interesting day. The directions in the route book said, "Right turn in front of the sign, *Reforma Constituyentes*." Okay, no problem there. Next it said, "Footbridge with sign, *Alencastre*

Periferico". The sign I saw was a little different, but I figured it had to be the right one. I warned Fritz that .4 kilometers after that sign, we would turn right toward *Periferico*. We came to a major intersection with a *Periferico* sign and I said, "Turn Right!"

Fritz had a hard time hearing me, even without his helmet and the engine noise, so I had to repeat myself a little louder. By this time we were entering the intersection. He yelled, "Here?"

I yelled back, "Yes!" thinking we would have to turn around, since we were already halfway through the intersection. Fritz, however, took me a little too literally and turned right on the wrong side of the median into oncoming traffic. Since there was a divider too tall to run over, he couldn't just cut across to the right side of the road. Fritz backed up into an on-ramp and turned around, only to find Tim coming at us head on in his El Camino. We took the next exit, which also said *Periferico*, but lost Tim in the confusion. We blasted down the street, trying to get somewhere, anywhere, while I used the siren to warn people of our approach. We hoped that Tim, who was nowhere in sight, wasn't doomed to wander forever the maze of streets in Mexico City.

While I was wondering what fate would befall Tim, Fritz was fairly annoyed that we were lost again. It wasn't long, though, before we found ourselves in the middle of a pack of race cars, actually about ten cars ahead of our starting position. Soon we were out of the city, motoring along the open highway behind another '54 Lincoln, a '54 Chevy, and a '55 Buick.

We decided to follow that pack of cars for a while, paying close attention to the route book. We had to maintain an average of 65 mph to the check point, but Fritz would occasionally run it up to around 100 just for the fun of it. We passed the Chrysler Assembly Plant of Mexico in

Toluca, and continued on to a toll booth. I hadn't thought to get change in Mexico City, so I handed Fritz a 20,000 *peso* note, roughly the equivalent of $8.70 in U.S. dollars, and told him to be sure to get change. He was too engrossed in the race to care about the denomination of the bill I gave him, so he just took what the attendant gave him and left. He handed me a few coins, and as the toll had only been 1300 *pesos*, I asked where the rest of the money was. The attendant had given him change for 2000 *pesos*, not 20,000 *pesos*, stiffing us for about $7.80. Well, these people are not exactly wealthy, so you can't blame them too much for taking advantage of the situation. The problem was that when we got to the next toll booth, I didn't have any more *pesos* for the toll. We gave the guy a dollar, knowing it would be more than enough to cover the 1200 *peso* toll. This attendant wanted more money, so rather than argue and waste more time, Fritz gave him another dollar. Either he didn't know the current exchange rate or he thought we were a couple of rich *gringos* who just fell off the tamale wagon, because he wanted more money.

Fritz looked at him and said, "No, we have to get going," and took off. After all, we'd already over paid him by 3300 *pesos*, and even in Mexico, *pesos* don't grow on trees. Nonetheless, when I looked behind us, I was relieved that we weren't being chased by the *Federales*.

It wasn't all fun and games though. We came across one of the other competitors, an orange '54 Mercury, mashed and mangled upside down on the hillside. Help had already arrived and there was nothing we could do, so we pressed on. We learned later that fortunately neither the driver nor co-driver where injured in the accident. We reached the first checkpoint where many of the other cars were parked, awaiting their desired departure time. This being a rally, the competitors were supposed to cross the checkpoint at an exact time interval after the car's starting time. For example, we left at 7:28:30, and with an exact two-hour interval being desired, we needed to cross the checkpoint at exactly 9:28:30. Since most of the cars, including us, had arrived about a half an hour early, we spent the time checking out our car and visiting with the other competitors.

After leaving the checkpoint, the rest of the morning passed smoothly. We came to the speed section for that day's leg, which was a winding mountain road with a few, shall we say, interesting turns. Since we had our kids in the back seat, complete with seat belts and crash helmets, Fritz took the turns considerably slower than if he had been alone, but we still made pretty good time. The scheduled lunch stop was at the *Plaza des Toros* (bullfighting arena) in Queretaro. We signed autographs, ate tacos, looked around, talked with some of the other drivers, and continued to wonder about Tim. Shortly, before we were scheduled to leave we heard the El Camino's vacuum operated 'wolf whistle.' Tim had managed to retrace his steps and find another Lincoln's support vehicle and follow him.

So, with one less thing to be concerned about, we left Queretaro and headed the 103 miles to Leon, the end of that day's leg. As we neared the city, the roads were thronged with people, waving, cheering, and blowing kisses. The closer we got to the city, the narrower the corridor for the race cars became. The enthusiastic crowd wanted to touch the car, touch my hand as we drove through. This wasn't particularly brilliant on my part to accommodate them, as I nearly dislocated my shoulder in the process, but we were all caught up in the moment.

We parked our car in the impound area, an open air pavilion about a block away from the Hotel Real Las Minas. We got out of the car only to discover a distressing green puddle growing under the radiator of the Lincoln. A cursory (accent on curse) examination revealed a pinhole in the radiator, no doubt caused by a small rock being thrown up as we came into town. Fritz assured me he could fix the leaky radiator without undue trouble, but Dan had a more serious problem. He had overheated his engine and the Copacabana had water coming out one of its exhaust pipes. Dan had been talking to one of our fellow competitors, who offered us the use of his shop there in Leon.

As these arrangements were being made, I decided it was time to take my two tired kids and check into the hotel. Once again I was greeted with, "You're who? How do you spell that? Do you have a car in the race?" After several minutes of trying to explain in broken Spanish and listening to their replies in broken English, I finally convinced them we belonged there and obtained a room for the night. Fritz and I then decided that since that night's party/ awards banquet was within walking distance of our hotel, that we would go and enjoy ourselves.

Dan, meanwhile, had taken his car over to the repair shop, and went to bed, feeling as 'wiped out' as the front of the Merc looked. Fritz, Tim, the kids and I got cleaned up and meandered over to the party. One of the honored guests was Luis Lozano of Guadalajara. He and Fritz hit it off quite well, as they were both enamored with Model A and T Fords, as well as vintage cars in general. He gave us his card and offered us the use of his restoration shop any time we were in Guadalajara. Pity we hadn't known him a few days earlier when we were trying to bang the Gopher Cabana back into shape. The only two problems with the party were 1) everything was announced in Spanish, meaning I could only understand about a tenth of what was said, and 2) they didn't eat dinner until 11:00. While this is a fairly common practice in Mexico, it's a little late for a tired California *gringa*. Around midnight I took my sleepy children to bed, and Fritz and Tim went off to repair our radiator and see what could be done for the Mercury.

The Copacabana required changing both head gaskets, replacing the points, plugs, and condenser, and checking out a multitude of other problems. While they were charging the Mercury's batteries, they both fell asleep - Tim in his El Camino with the engine running and Fritz lying on a piece of cardboard under the car. Praise the Lord it was not a fully enclosed shop. Carbon monoxide is not your friend. Finally they woke up enough to stumble over to the impound area, put some epoxy on the Lincoln's radiator, then stumble into our room for a couple of hours sleep. I was not terribly amused that my husband dragged his backside into our room at 5 a.m., after having spent a restless night playing out numerous scenarios in my head. These ranged from alcohol bearing *senoritas* to gun bearing *banditos*, all of which were pretty unlikely in the light of day, but seemed very plausible in the middle of the night.

When I was finally able to drag Fritz and Tim out of bed, Fritz decided that he had better fill the tank on the Lincoln before we started that day's leg. As soon as the water in the radiator of the Lincoln warmed up it melted the epoxy, which hadn't had enough time to cure, and the leak reopened. Dan was also having problems with the Merc. He had borrowed an ignition coil to replace the one that had gone bad in his car, but the Copacabana still wouldn't start. Due to both of these temporary setbacks, and the fact that the race cars were lining up to leave, we decided to forego that day's leg of the race, repair our race cars, and catch up with the rest of the pack in Zacatecas.

We took the Mercury and the Lincoln back to the shop. Fritz removed the radiator from the Lincoln and walked down the street, radiator in hand to a local radiator repair shop. The proprietor repaired the leak, and naturally wanted to test his work. He didn't have an air compressor or a test tank in which to submerge it, so he did the next best thing. He plugged both water outlets, filled the radiator with water, and had his young apprentice, a boy of about ten, put his mouth over the filler neck and blow as hard as he could. That kid must have had quite a lung capacity Fritz said his checks were bulged out so far he thought they were going to burst.

Meanwhile, Tim, the kids, and I had something more pressing on our minds - finding breakfast and some fresh, cold milk. We had passed a truck unloading some bottles of milk on a little side street on the way to the shop, so we decided to go in search of it. We went up and down a multitude of back alleys and one way streets, although not always the right way, I might add. We stopped at corner markets, bakeries, anywhere that even remotely looked like it might have milk, but to no avail. I later learned through Elisa's translations that there was a severe milk shortage in the area. We did, however, find some really tasty fresh doughnuts for about a nickel each. So, having finally given up on the search for milk, we made our way back to the shop, only getting lost a few times in the process.

Fritz and Dan, meanwhile, were discussing what needed to be done to the Mercury. In all honesty, that poor little supercharged flathead was in sad shape. Throughout the journey, both the Merc's batteries and its maze of wiring had proven less than satisfactory. The good news was that the drive shaft driven alternator was working. The bad news was there was still a drain on the system somewhere. Dan, trying not to drain his batteries, had not run his electric fans while sitting in heavy traffic and overheated the engine, cracking the block. Actually, at that point I think we were all a little cracked. Even with the new head gaskets, water was still pouring out the exhaust pipes. We decided to try some Mexican Permatex block sealer. This particular variety isn't available in the states - I think the EPA has some issues with its chemical composition. We had to remove four of the spark plugs and pour it straight into the block, unlike other types that go into the engine through the radiator. Amazingly enough, considering the extent of the damage, the operation was quite successful. After that, we drained the emulsified oil, which resembled a weak chocolate malt, and replaced it with something that looked more like motor oil. We also bought two new Champion coils - one to replace the less than satisfactory coil that Dan had borrowed, and one for a spare. Fritz had already reinstalled our kid tested radiator, so we were finally ready to head toward Zacatecas.

About 25 miles out of Leon, Tim realized he had left his camera back at the shop where we had been working. We decided to wait for him at the next wide spot in the road while he went back to look for it. After pulling over, Fritz, being exhausted in more ways than one from his night in the shop under the cars, promptly put his head in my lap and went to sleep. I tried to keep our two restless kids quiet, and after a while started to wonder if Tim was encountering a new problem. About the time Fritz woke up and we turned around to go look for Tim, he showed up, triumphantly clutching his camera in his upraised hand. Our little band together again, we once more headed toward Zacatecas.

We stopped for gas and noticed a small café next door. While the doughnuts had been tasty, they didn't really stick with us, so the overwhelming consensus was to eat. This place must have been a favorite of the local truckers, as there were large collages of photographs featuring many of the trucks that frequented the place, complete with "Ben Hur" spikes coming from the wheels.

By the time we resumed our journey it was getting dark. To save Dan's electrical system any more strain, we towed the Mercury behind the Lincoln. Fritz had to keep waking me up so that I, in turn, could keep him awake. I had just drifted off for the umpteenth time when suddenly Fritz slammed on the brakes and did a little fancy maneuvering with the steering wheel. Directly in front of us were three trucks. The second truck had run into the first, which had come to a dead stop in the middle of the highway - no lights, no flares, no warning of any kind. The third truck had slammed on his brakes to avoid hitting the other two. Fritz had four options - swerve into oncoming traffic, which was plentiful; take the ditch, which was very steep and probably would have rolled both cars; hit the truck, bashing our front end and probably us in the process; or jack knife the Copacabana. Since I'm alive to tell this story, obviously he chose the latter, thinking it would cause the least damage to the cars and their occupants. The Gopher Cabana probably got a bit more damage, which in light of its previous experience in Guadalajara was fairly inconsequential. The right rear quarter panel of the Lincoln was definitely crumpled, which made the scratch and ding from the lady before we crossed the border pretty negligible. Immediately Fritz and Tim threw down a couple of flares and started to work on unhooking the tow bar and realigning the cars so we could get out of the middle of the road. The trucks that had caused this mess, meanwhile, had resolved their own problems and driven off, leaving us to our own devices.

It was late at night when we finally reached race headquarters in Zacatecas. Amazingly enough, I didn't have any problems with our hotel reservations that night. Perhaps the Lord thought I had been through enough that day. Dan and Elisa's hotel turned out to be on the other side of town, so Tim drove them there in the El Camino. At last we were all able to get a little rest.

Since Dan and Elisa's hotel was on the other side of town, the plan was for Tim to tow their car to them in the morning in time for them to get to the starting line. For some obscure reason we went with Tim in search of their hotel. Race time was near when Tim spotted it, so Fritz and I decided we had better get back or we'd miss another day's start. Once again we weren't sure where we were supposed to go, and ended up going about three miles out of our way before finally finding the starting line with five minutes to spare.

When we got there, we found Dan jumping up and down wondering where his car was. He and Elisa had gotten a ride with some race officials, and had missed Tim entirely. Since Tim couldn't find Dan at the hotel, he found the starting line in the nick of time, with about four cars to go - including us - before it was Dan and Elisa's turn to take off.

We left from downtown Zacatecas, winding through the very old narrow streets, which were about the size of a narrow alley. At one point, a turn was so sharp and so narrow that the Lincoln wouldn't bend around it, so Fritz had to back up and re-angle the car to make the corner. After winding through a few more crowd lined streets, we made our way out of town and onto the open highway.

We were happy to see that the orange '54 Mercury was back in the race. It was still a bit haggard looking from its experience a few days earlier, but had been beaten more or less back into shape. We cruised along until we reached one of the morning's checkpoints where the cars were to stop and wait. There seemed to be mass confusion as to who was going when, etc. A combination of race cars, sightseers, and everyday traffic was jamming the road

Diary of a Racer's Wife

in both directions, as bad as a California freeway during rush hour. Fritz and I were behind about a dozen cars, waiting our turn. I told him by my clock, we were supposed to leave in 45 seconds, but considering the traffic and congestion, I didn't know what we could do about it. Fritz, as usual, had his own method of dealing with such situations. He drove the Lincoln down the embankment into the ditch, roaring around the cars that were in our way, and then came up back onto the road, while I had the siren wailing the whole time. We reached the starting line with a few seconds to spare, then took off. The officials did seem somewhat surprised to see a 4400 pound Lincoln flying up out of the ditch toward them.

That day's lunch stop was at Durango, a very friendly, enthusiastic town. After lunch, Andy decided he wanted to ride in the El Camino with Tim, so it was just Fritz, Jason and I in the Lincoln. We were drifting through a corner at about 60 mph when we saw a mangled silver Porsche off to the right in the bushes. We later learned it had hit a bus and spun out. A Mexican observer described it as a wounded chinchilla scurrying into the underbrush. Help was once again already there, so we continued on our journey.

We were discussing the accident when we noticed some people near some large rocks on the cliff ahead. We didn't think much about it until a boulder approximately three feet in diameter came crashing down the hillside toward the road directly in front of us. It was one of those situations where time seems to slow down for a moment - I could see Fritz thinking, calculating what he had to do to miss it. He was able to adjust the car's speed and swerve, barely missing the boulder. Had they pushed it just a fraction of a second later, it could easily have crashed through the roof of the car and killed all three of us. I don't know what they were thinking - whether

76

they just wanted to scare us, or see if they could kill us, or what. Sometimes people do odd things. I did at that moment wonder what I had been thinking, bringing my children down here. The reality, though, is that I had thought I had a reliable babysitter when I left home. And even though that didn't work out, once Fritz was committed to something, he was committed, and turning back was never a real option.

It was mid-afternoon when we reached Torreon. I hadn't realized it was such a large city. We were directed to the community center, which was to be the impound area. The owner of the local Ford dealership told Fritz in Spanish that he would be happy to change the oil in the Lincoln and give it a complete service. Once Fritz understood what he was saying, he politely declined, saying he always serviced his own vehicles. The owner of the Chevy dealership also offered the use of his facilities to the racers, and several of them decided to take him up on his offer. The silver Porsche we had seen in the bushes arrived at impound a short time later on a trailer, complete with the black rubber imprint of a 1000-22 Firestone across its rear quarter.

After hanging around the impound area for a few hours, we found someone to lead us to our hotel, the El Presidente. Neither Dan nor Tim had arrived at the impound area while we were there, nor were they at the hotel when we arrived. I was becoming concerned. Tim had my seven-year-old son with him, and I didn't relish the thought of him being stranded somewhere in Mexico. Well, Tim either, for that matter, but my immediate thoughts were of Andy. Fritz convinced me we needed to wait before going in search of them. We checked in with only minimal difficulty and were given two bottles of the local wine. Our room overlooked the parking lot, so we sat there sipping wine and watching for signs of my son.

Diary of a Racer's Wife

We dozed off, concerned and exhausted - I was concerned, Fritz was exhausted - but the rest of the troupe, including Andy, eventually arrived.

The next morning, shortly before it was time to leave for the starting line, Fritz decided we had better get some gas. I gave him what should have been enough money and he headed up the street. A few minutes later, the Lincoln came screaming back into the parking lot, with Fritz shouting, "Give me some money, quick!" Realizing I could save time by digging through my purse for money on the way, I threw the kids in the car and hopped in, and we blasted up the street. We normally used half *extra* (unleaded premium) and half *nova* (regular leaded). Since gas prices were standardized in Mexico, I knew to the *peso* what that should cost. The attendant had put in extra *"extra"* however, and Fritz had to leave our 35 mm camera there as collateral until we could return and cover the additional charge. We paid the man, retrieved the camera, and returned to the hotel to collect Tim and Dan. By this time we were running late, but once again Dan's fluency in Spanish paid off and he was able to get decent directions to the starting line. It was, however, a good thing we always started toward the back of the pack, or we would have had a problem.

In the few minutes we had waiting at the starting line, an older gentleman began telling me (in English) of his memories of the original Pan Am races. He was very pleased to see them being run again, as were many of the people we spoke with. It brought back memories of a more innocent age, for him, and I enjoyed our conversation. Soon it was our turn to go. While we waited for our final countdown, an elderly lady traditionally dressed in a *rebozo* shawl smiled, said a prayer for us and blessed us. Then we sped off.

The road was beginning to straighten out more

and more. During the transit stage, when we weren't required to wear our helmets, I slid over in the seat next to Fritz. Fritz then suggested that I drive for a while. I enthusiastically agreed. How many chances does a California housewife get to drive in the La Carrera Panamericana? Not wanting to waste time pulling over, we performed our changing places without pulling over maneuver, a tricky little procedure requiring Fritz to keep his foot on the gas while I slid over him and under the steering wheel. Some of the other racers did give some odd looks as we did this, but we'd had experience in some of our other ventures. Fritz was never one to waste time by pulling over when going somewhere.

I drove at a sensible speed of around 75 mph until we came to the next checkpoint. It was a strange feeling, not being the navigator - I was the one who was used to knowing where we were going. At the checkpoint, we traded positions again and took off for the speed stage. This speed stage, like a number of those previous, was on winding roads. Poor Fritz - I could see him calculating how fast he could be taking each turn if he was alone. However, he had his family with him, and some common sense had to prevail. He was still able to be competitively fast, though.

Our lunch stop for this leg was in Paral, where the people seemed determined to outdo all the other towns. A local girls club had made ham sandwiches for the racers. The people were friendly, wanting autographs, asking questions about the kids, etc. The kids, as usual, were crowd pleasers, eliciting the usual *"Que bonito!"* and *"Que precioso!"* In the crush of the crowd we didn't notice the rest of the race cars leaving ahead of us. Finally realizing that the crowd was all hanging around us and the Mercury because the other cars were gone, we jumped in our cars with a hearty *"Adios amigos!"* and made our way to the checkpoint with a minute or so to spare.

By this point in the race, Fritz and I had become reasonably accomplished at getting to the checkpoints at the proper time. There were several times when the official's watch was completely different from our rally clock, but you have to expect that kind of thing. During the timed "limited" stages there was an internal checkpoint where you could get extra points for being a certain amount of time early - usually ten minutes - within the desired total elapsed time. There was a penalty, of course, if you were too early or too late. Our biggest problem was Fritz had difficulty driving slowly. I would calculate a speed to maintain, but occasionally I'd glance over and notice the speedometer needle creeping up and yell at him to slow down, then calculate a new speed. On the last "limited" internal checkpoint of this leg, we arrived ten seconds early, which I thought was pretty good, but Fritz moaned and said, "Why didn't you tell me sooner? I would have slowed down!"

We arrived in downtown Chihuahua that afternoon to complimentary Corona *cervezas*. I'm not that big of a drinker, but after a long, hot, dry ride, cold beer tasted pretty good. The lengthy procession of race cars began moving toward the hotels. We noticed that Dan and Elisa had pulled over, so we stopped to see if they needed help, thereby losing sight of the other race cars. Oh well, by that time I was used to being lost in Mexico. The Merc was having electrical problems, but Dan and Tim seemed to have the situation under control, so Fritz and I decided to resume our search for the hotel, which turned out to be the Chihuahua Hilton.

After they freshened up a bit, Fritz and Andy were interviewed by the local television station. We then took a bus to the awards dinner. Once again the people were absolutely wonderful. The mayor and the head of the city council came over to us and shook our hands, saying that if there was anything at all they could do for us we only had to ask. Never having had such an offer before, Fritz and I couldn't think of anything to ask for. During the awards presentation, Fritz and I were introduced as a "Marriage of Wheels", which in retrospect was relatively accurate. We ate an incredible roast beef dinner which was adequate, we were told by a local official, but unfortunately not their best - false modesty, no doubt, or else they have some seriously good beef down there, as I have never had its equal. Afterward we slowly walked back to the hotel in the cool desert night, anticipating the final day of racing.

In the morning we went next door to Dan's hotel to help get his car ready for the run to Ciudad Juarez. The race cars were scheduled to begin departing at 10:00. At 9:58, Fritz and I decided we had better get some gas and find the starting line. We couldn't find a gas station, so we had to forego that and get some after we took off - figuring we could easily make up the time. The only problem with that theory was that we couldn't find the starting line either. We drove frantically around Chihuahua for about 10 minutes, siren blaring, looking for some sign of the other racers. I would like to take a moment to clarify something, so that Fritz and I don't look like total idiots. Throughout the race, the route book usually, although not always accurately, gave the name of a landmark where the start was to be. At no time, however, did it give any directions as to how to get there. Can't have everything.

It looked like we were not going to make it this time. While we sat in frustration at a traffic signal, a Mexican gentleman asked me the time in Spanish. In desperation I cried, *"Donde esta la salida de la carrera?"* ("Where is the start of the race?") Quickly he drew us a map, explaining in Spanish and doing a lot of pointing. It was the pointing that saved us. Poor guy, I never did tell him what time it was. The light changed and we were off! The street we needed to be on had been closed down for the race, so we had to take a parallel street with a median between us and the racers. Fritz made a left turn in the middle of the street and drove up over the median into the midst of the remaining race cars. There were only a few cars ahead of us, and then away we went, once again making the start by the grace of God with seconds to spare.

A few blocks down the street we slid into a gas station, got gas, threw the attendant some money and roared off. After we caught up to the other cars, we resumed a more sensible speed.

The speed stage was only a few miles out of town. The officials, for some obscure reason known only to them, had chosen a winding abandoned road, with potholes big enough to lose a Porsche in. In retrospect, I don't recall seeing one of the VW bugs again after that section. It kind of makes you wonder. This particular stretch of road was so bad that the route book not only told you the intensity of the curves, but also the intensity of the potholes. We quickly but carefully picked our way through, being grateful for the new front shocks and thinking about the work we needed to do to the rear suspension.

After what seemed an eternity, even at high speed, we were through the speed stage and back on the main road. This was virtually a straight shot to Ciudad Juarez. We weren't supposed to do any passing on that leg, so that the cars could cross the finish line in their starting order. It also minimized the potentially dangerous high speed driving that could be done on that nice, straight, open road. This was equally difficult for Fritz and the Lincoln, as they both wanted to go faster.

We approached the last internal checkpoint of the race. I had carefully calculated and recalculated our time and speed. Fritz was holding the car's speed steady at 67.5 mph. The checkpoint was in sight. It looked like we were finally going to cross one at exactly the right time. Five hundred feet away from the checkpoint, the Lincoln coughed. It had run out of gas on the main tank. Fritz quickly switched to the auxiliary tank and increased our speed, but the delay had cost us six precious seconds. I couldn't feel too badly though - we still did better than a number of the other competitors, some of whom had expensive rally computers.

After that we were travelling toward Juarez on a string straight four lane highway. The racers couldn't hold it in any longer. We all put the pedal to the metal and sped toward the finish line. We passed a '54 Chevy from Newport Beach, California, holding our speed to a conservative 115. We were gaining on another Lincoln when the crowd started to thicken and we all had to slow down. We were nearing Juarez and the final finish line of the race when we allowed the cars we had passed to re-pass us, returning to our starting order as requested. As we came to a large crowd under a trestle, and passed by a man waving the checkered flag, Fritz excitedly asked, "Do you know who that is?" I, in my youthful innocence, had no clue. Fritz exclaimed, "That's Juan Fangio, the greatest race driver in the world!"

To which I replied, "Well, next to you, honey."

Traffic was heavy as we headed into town. Many of the spectators had brought out their vintage cars to be part of the spectacle. Up ahead of us we saw the '54 Corvette veer off and run up the curb. Fritz jumped out of the Lincoln and went over to see if he could help. It was determined that the brake pedal clevis pin had fallen out, rendering the brakes useless. At that point, Fritz decided to take a few pictures and let me cope with moving the Lincoln onward through the slow and go traffic.

Fortunately he returned to the car before I completely lost sight of him - I'd most definitely had enough of being lost for a while. We crossed under the finish structure which marked the entrance to the final display area. After parking in the display area, Fritz decided to return to the finish structure to photographically record the Juarez finish for posterity. In the last two La Carrera Classics Fritz had been unable to get a photo of the finish banner, and he decided nothing would stop him this time. He had just focused and was about to shoot when a large gust of wind came up. As the structure fell, sending people scurrying out of the way, Fritz snapped four consecutive shots of the end of another finish.

It was finally over. We were both relieved and saddened at the same time. After that, everything seemed anticlimactic. We decided to follow a group of about ten other cars to the hotel, which turned out to be the Hotel Lucerne, thinking it was nice not to be lost for once. We changed our minds, however, when our whole procession had to turn around on a dead end street. Apparently the lead car didn't know where he was going, either.

We only got a little lost on our way to the awards dinner that night. The only awards given out were for the Mexican drivers. The rest of us had to be content with picking up a trophy after the ceremony was over and getting our finishing order the following day. It was a pleasure meeting Fangio, however, and he held Jason and gave him a kiss on the cheek.

The next day we were informed that we had finished fourth among the Americans and 14th overall. Considering that we had only raced officially four of the eight days - Pueblo didn't count- we thought we had done pretty well.

Around 4:30 that afternoon, we headed for the border, towing the Merc. On the last day of racing, Dan had overheated the poor crispy little flathead to 270 degrees, which is not a happy temperature for that type of engine, or most other types, for that matter. As for the Lincoln, we were developing some weak valve springs and knew that we had some serious suspension work to do before the next race. As we faced the 700 or so mile trip home, I turned to Fritz and said, "You know, life with you isn't always easy, but it's never boring."

"Dangerous Curves"

Chapter 7

Racing Isn't Always a Bowl of Cherries

During the off season, we used the Lincoln as everyday transportation. As such, painted in its "road race regalia", it definitely attracted attention every time we drove it. One memorable morning we were on our way to Temecula through De Luz when a couple of Border Patrol officers noticed us and decided to check us out. Fritz thought it could be great fun and put the accelerator to the floor, being extremely familiar with both the canyon and the Lincoln's capabilities. This caught the Border Patrol by surprise, and they took off after us in hot pursuit. After a couple of miles, much to my relief, Fritz pulled over to wait for them, deciding they could get hurt if they tried too hard to keep us with us. The Border Patrol car came screaming around the corner, saw us and slammed on the brakes, pulling in behind us. As they came up to the window, more than a little confused, Fritz sort of apologized, saying he was just having fun with them.

One of them asked, "Man, what do you have in this thing?" My errant racer told them it was a slightly modified Lincoln engine, and that we road raced in Mexico. The officer said, "Well, since you've pulled over, do you mind if we take a look in your trunk?" Obviously, his thought was to make sure we weren't smuggling undocumented immigrants, but he did seem somewhat surprised to see a thirty-gallon fuel cell mounted back there. Before they headed back to their vehicle, one of them said something to the effect of, "Well, drive safe". We continued on toward Temecula at a more sedate pace - well, sedate is a relative term when you're talking about Fritz. Personally, I was extremely relieved those guys had a sense of humor.

In late February of '89, our friend Rick Martin decided to come out from a cold, snowy Ohio to a less cold, rainy Southern California to help us prepare for the upcoming La Carrera Classic, as well as being Fritz's co-driver during the race. Rick, who is something of a guru of road race Lincolns, quickly proved himself invaluable in helping prepare the car. In reality, Fritz was very hands on even when it came to other people's work, and the fact that he let Rick work on the transmission without clucking over him like a nervous hen was both a testament to his faith in Rick and a bit of a minor miracle. Fritz was dividing his time between trying to build another engine for Dan's Mercury and getting a set of 368 heads ready to install on the Lincoln's 317 engine. During the previous year's Pan Am, we had burnt at least one exhaust valve and couldn't readily obtain a replacement. In addition, Fritz was helping his sister Jeanie care for their father, Lonnie, who was dying of cancer.

Lonnie passed away on March 1st, two days before we were to leave for the race. Fritz's best solution for grief was to throw himself into his work and go racing. His worst solution was to get drunk. I've seen both and I liked the work solution better. I felt as if we would be abandoning Jeanie, but all of the arrangements for Lonnie had already been made, and Fritz was determined to go racing. Due to other complications, Dan chose to run his BMW instead of the Merc, which was a relief to Fritz as it gave him more time for the Lincoln.

Diary of a Racer's Wife

By Friday the Lincoln was back together. Our friends Barry and Sandy, who had agreed to crew for us again this year, got to the ranch at around 11:00. We loaded up camping equipment, tools, kids, and so on, and headed to Escondido to check on Jim T.'s progress with his '54 Lincoln convertible, then went to K-Mart to buy a pair of rear shocks for our Lincoln. To the amazement of the mechanics watching them from K-Mart's auto center, Fritz and Rick quickly installed them in the parking lot. I overheard one of them making a comment about it to the manager, and he said, "Yeah, these racers are pretty darned quick." We made a stop at the market for provisions, and were off across the border to Estero Beach.

As we were running late (Who, us? What a shock!), we went straight to where we had been told the drivers' meeting was going to be held, only to find it wasn't there. Fritz and I figured we had a good idea of what was being said anyway, so we didn't worry about it too much, although it would have been nice for Rick's sake. Our little group proceeded to the race headquarters hotel, where Fritz and Rick signed in. Afterwards, they had a few final adjustments to make on the Lincoln in the chilly night air before we could set up the tent and turn in for the night. While I loved Ensenada and the La Carrera Classic, I admit I had gotten somewhat spoiled by all of the hotels during the Pan Am, and the tent had lost its luster.

The following morning we rose early, ate breakfast, and started preparing for the day's events. We had recently purchased a used video camera in the hopes of recording the race, but it decided not to work, so we were back to the old reliable 35 mm film camera, which also chose not to work. Fritz was finally able to get it functioning again at least, but it did seem to be an inauspicious start to the day ahead.

Before going into Ensenada for the 'false start' of the

race, Fritz and Rick circled around to race headquarters, where they found Jim, who had made it down with his ragtop Lincoln just in time. They let him know what was going on, and caravanned back into town.

Fritz and Rick started mid pack this year, with Jim close behind. Their fearless pit crew arrived just in time to see them off as they honked and waved, with cheers following them through Ensenada to the 10 K marker and the official start of the race. After the remaining racers left, we headed out to the starting line to await the re-opening of the road. It was a refreshing change to not get lost on the way there.

Less than a mile from the start we came across a green Morgan that had apparently rolled, although it was unclear why it happened on that particular stretch of road. The situation was under control, though, and there were no major injuries, so we were able to continue on.

Meanwhile, Fritz and Rick were zipping through the mountains, tires squealing around the corners, passing several cars. Rick told me later that no one could keep up with them through the mountains. Having spent a lot of time riding with Fritz in our own canyon, I easily believed him. Once they were past the mountains and onto the straightaways, their problems began. The Lincoln, which had always run up to 130 mph without hesitation, refused to exceed 105.

There was supposed to be a warning sign and a cone a half mile before the pit stop, another cone and a flagman a quarter of a mile before it, and another flag-man at the pit entrance. This was planned to assure that no cars would miss the pit stop as they had in previous years. Remember what they say about the best laid plans of mice, men and racers? The reality was that there were no cones and no extra flagman - no warning of any kind. When the flagman literally jumped out in front of Fritz, he had to hit the brakes hard and slide sideways to avoid hitting him, and then proceed to the pits. On a side note, when Jim arrived at the pit stop a few minutes later, the flagman was standing on a rock, well away from the side of the road. I guess almost being run down by one 4400 pound Lincoln made him hesitant to try that again.

The pit stop went relatively well, although there was some confusion among the timers of the race. Fritz and Rick made sure they left on time, however, as the poor Lincoln wasn't running fast enough to compensate for any mistakes.

The adjustments they made during the pit stop seemed to worsen the car's performance. After debating whether to continue at a slow pace or take the time to pull over and try to improve the situation, Fritz and Rick chose the latter to adjust the carburetor float levels and the timing. They reached the conclusion during these exercises that our poor old stock fuel pump, which had given us thousands of miles of faithful service, was weary from all the high speed driving. After this realization, Fritz and Rick had to settle back to an all too leisurely drive to the finish line.

Their problems paled in comparison to what happened to others. Fritz and Rick came across a burning Porsche upside down at the side of the road. The driver had been seriously injured and flown to San Diego for medical attention, and his wife, who was his co-driver, had been killed instantly. Fritz and Rick were waved on, so they continued down the road to the next tragedy.

In a particularly nasty series of turns near the end of the race, the same location a Camaro had crashed in the '87 La Carrera Classic, Fritz and Rick once again saw an ominous cloud of smoke from a burning car. This time it was a Pantera, and the sole occupant had lost his life, probably on impact. Soon after that sobering sight, our

Lincoln crossed the finish line. Fritz was frustrated by our car's performance, and naturally concerned for those involved in the accidents, and our hearts went out to their families. Barry, Sandy, the kids and I arrived an hour or so later, and we all proceeded to the race headquarters hotel, the Castel.

It had been chilly in Ensenada and San Felipe was no warmer. Due to the cool temperatures and somber atmosphere, the end of race party and awards dinner, which were held outside, were dismal failures. I believe the word "fiasco" applies. We were unable to learn our average speed that evening, but in light of everything that had happened we weren't too concerned about it anyway. We spent the night in the campground next to the hotel and hoped that the next day would be better. It's safe to say that we've had better races.

Before we headed back to California, we learned our average had been just over 82 mph, putting us second in our class behind a '54 Chrysler. Fritz, ever the good sport, philosophically commented, "Well, we have to let somebody else win once in a while." This race was definitely a sobering reminder that racing is a dangerous sport and should not be entered into lightly.

The 1989 racing season continued for us, though - El Mirage and Bonneville, with the Antique Nationals thrown in for good measure. We considered returning to the Pan Am in the fall, but decided it just wasn't in the cards this time. I'm not sure we had fully recovered from last time, and the Lincoln definitely needed some attention. This year Fritz decided to build a 750 cc KR engine to put in the KH chassis for Bonneville, calling it "Full House Mouse 3." He talked our friend Keenan into going to the salt with us for the first time, which must have been a good experience for him, because he returned with his own bikes many times after that, and set numerous records. That year we achieved a speed of just over 90 mph. Granted it was nothing to get too excited about considering the potential of a KR engine, but at least we kept it together. The thing I remember most about that particular Speed Week had little to do with the bike, however. Fritz had a way of ordering me around and expecting me to do what he said, which, as his wife and crew chief, I did. When Keenan tried that however, I told him I wasn't his wife and I wasn't his girlfriend, so if he wanted something he needed to say please and thank you. He's been polite to me ever since, which I still appreciate. We did go on that season to set two records with the KR at El Mirage - one in October and the second in November. After El Mirage, racing season was over for a few months, and I was looking forward to some long winter evenings next to the fire.

Chapter 8
Bouncing Back in Baja

Silly me, even though Fritz and I had known about the 1990 La Carrera Classic coming up in March, we had other obligations and I thought we had decided to shelve the idea, and participate in another race that was supposed to be coming up in May. Three days before the race, however, Fritz, making sure I was listening, was telling his friend Jim over the phone that we'd been married so long that I didn't ever want to do anything anymore, that I didn't like racing, and that basically I was becoming an old hag at the age of 28. So, to uphold my reputation as the supportive wife of a "racing fool," as Fritz had been called by at least one of his friends, I told him if he felt that way about it we should go. Fritz immediately called Loyal, the American coordinator for the race and negotiated the price a bit since we wouldn't be using the hotel included in San Felipe. He then drove up to Whittier to help his mother for the day. Meanwhile I started packing and tried to figure out who we could get for a pit crew on extremely short notice.

Fritz had repaired the Lincoln's fuel pump problem from the year before, so this year we were hoping to have a little better showing at the La Carrera Classic. I will say this about the old fuel pump - in spite of the fact that the diaphragm spring was broken in literally six pieces and the rubber diaphragm itself was cracked, it pumped gas right to the end. I'm kind of surprised Fritz didn't build a monument to it. He didn't have time to change the rear brake shoes, but he was never too concerned about driving without brakes anyway. Not that this has anything to do with racing, but we did drive the Lincoln the 500 miles home from Santa Cruz with only an emergency brake. Fortunately, it only got exciting a couple of times. Have I mentioned that I pray a lot?

Finding a pit crew was our next challenge. Barry and Sandy couldn't make it this time, but we did find a couple of friends who were able to get time off work to help us - Greg and Jim C. We were to supply the support vehicle and the gas. To save wear and tear and gas, we decided to tow my Chevy Luv truck behind the Lincoln. I realize most people tow their race vehicle behind their support vehicle, but this was definitely the better choice, and Fritz and I were never exactly defined as "normal".

Fritz, Andy, Jason and I left Friday morning only one hour later than we had intended - which for us bordered on absolutely amazing. We drove up to Ramona to pick up Jim, then to the train station in San Diego to pick up Greg. We made a quick supply stop at the market and an auto parts store for an air cleaner. Fritz had been contemplating buying a radiator cap as well, but decided $4.79 was an exorbitant amount and it wasn't essential. This accomplished, we headed across the border for the hour long drive to Ensenada.

When we arrived at race headquarters shortly after noon, my first thought was that we were in the wrong place because of the lack of people milling around. There were only around 30 entries, but the smaller group created more of a family type atmosphere.

The race format was a little different than it had been in the three previous La Carrera Classics we had attended, as there was to be a hill climb that afternoon up to La Bufadora (the blowhole). The speeds achieved during the hill climb would determine the starting order for Saturday's race. Another change was that the race itself would only be run flat out to Independencia, and after that it would be run as a rally. This meant that at certain times the racers had to maintain a certain average speed instead of driving as fast as they wanted, like we had done in the Pan Am a few years earlier. There were also areas of bad road that were transit stages, when your time and speed were unimportant. Fritz wanted to do the hill climb and the speed stage alone, and I would join him in Independencia to navigate for the remainder of the race. The reason for this change, of course, was to slow the cars down in the straightaways where last year's fatal accidents had occurred.

After paying our entry, getting teched and doing a little bench racing, we decided to go out to the blow hole and pre-run the course. Fritz, Jason and I took off up the hill, which was still open to traffic, leaving Greg, Jim, and eight-year-old Andy in the dust. The road was a winding gradual uphill grade, and although it was paved, it wasn't exactly what you would call smooth. Once he had an idea of what to expect, we returned to race headquarters to kick tires with the other racers until it was time for the hill climb.

Before the road was actually closed, Jim, Greg, the kids and I climbed into the mini truck, which was no mean feat considering how much we had it loaded, and drove about three quarter way up the course so we could watch the cars going by at speed. The cars were released at 30 second intervals. A Ferrari Dino flew past, only to leave most of his oil in a puddle at the top of the hill. The Lincoln handled beautifully, as usual. There was a '56 Olds that kind of resembled a sow wallowing in the mud on its way up - definitely some suspension issues.

Diary of a Racer's Wife

At the drivers meeting that night the main emphasis was to have a safe race, which was understandable after last year's unfortunate events. While we were watching a slide show put together by one of the participants in the previous year's Pan Am, the owner of the Ferrari Dino walked in carrying the aluminum sump plate off his car's oil pan. It had a crack the width of it, as well as a hole, which explained the oil at the top of La Bufadora. He explained he had bottomed out and hit a rock in the road on the way up. He was somewhat frantically trying to locate a welding shop in Ensenada with heliarc facilities to repair the aluminum plate. As the poor Dino owner was having little success, Fritz casually told him over his shoulder to bring it back to the pits after the drivers meeting and he would oxy-acetylene weld it, which isn't particularly suitable for aluminum. This was met with a good deal of disbelief, but desperate times call for desperate measures and the Dino owner agreed. So after the meeting, Fritz, having no available aluminum filler rod, used a piece of coat hanger to stir the puddle of existing aluminum and very carefully filled the hole and repaired the damaged area. Not something most people could do, but Ferrari used good aluminum and Fritz was an amazing man.

The highway to San Felipe was supposed to close at 8:00 a.m., so around 7:30 Greg, Jim, the kids and I piled in the Luv truck and headed into Ensenada. Greg then told us he had to find a phone so he could call work and get the day off. He worked for Union Pacific Railroad, which would only give him 24 hours off at a time. Having had some experience with Mexican telephones, especially trying to get through to Omaha, Nebraska where the railroad's home office was located, I was prepared to panic over the amount of time it would take to get through. It took considerable driving through Ensenada and three

96

phones to accomplish this. I felt kind of like Goldilocks - the first phone was too broken, the second the operator cut him off and never came back, but the third one was just right. By this time it was 8:30, a half hour after the road was supposed to be closed. We high tailed it through town without getting lost - I felt like I was finally getting the hang of this - and made it past the checkpoint toward Independencia before the *Federales* closed the road. Some course stewards were putting markers at the curves to warn the race drivers of their severity - '1' for bad, '2' for worse, and '3' for slow down, idiot. We played leapfrog with them for 10 or 15 miles. They'd stop to put out a marker and we would pass them, they'd finish, zoom around us and wave, we'd wave as they stopped to put out another marker, etc.

Meanwhile, back in Ensenada, Fritz was waiting around at the false start of the race, passing out Pick-A-Part screwdrivers and propaganda to the other racers. He had ranked 13th in the hill climb, starting behind an Alfa Romeo. The crowd cheered him on as he motored through town and to the official starting line at the 10 K marker.

We didn't have long to wait in Independencia before the first car came in - the Dino Ferrari. Around seventh or eighth Fritz came flying in, turning a brodie, and scaring Jim half to death when he saw the Lincoln sliding toward him. He said, "Geez, I didn't know you guys brought me down here to try to kill me!"

A minute or two later, Fritz eventually came to a stop and backed up to the officials at the checkpoint. About that time, I jumped in and asked him how it went. He told me that on one of the last straightaways the Stewart Warner speedometer indicated 135 mph. He said that while it felt like it had more to give, he didn't want to hurt the poor old girl and backed off to around 125.

Andy stayed with Jim, and Greg wanted to ride in

the Lincoln with Fritz and me. Jason, being two, didn't have a say in the matter - he rode with me. We drove the mile down the road to where the other race cars were congregated. The driver and navigator of the Bug-eyed Sprite approached us and asked if they could borrow/buy some gas from us, so naturally we gave them some. During the course of our conversation the driver told me, "Fritz came flying around us at a ridiculous rate of speed. I thought we were travelling in reverse!" He also told us that the Pick-A-Part screwdriver Fritz had given him before the race had saved them. During the speed stage their fuel filter had clogged up. Having no other tools with them, they used the screwdriver to disassemble the filter and punch enough holes in it to continue the race.

Having no official instruction at the time, and having been told at the driver's meeting that the transit stage didn't count for points, we left when the other cars did, helmets and seatbelts on, to the next checkpoint at Valle de la Trinidad where the timed "limited" stage began. Greg and I synchronized our watches. As we roared away, the '56 Olds was in front of us with their fancy, expensive rally equipment, so we began by hacking off them briefly while I worked out my computations with my less than fancy pen, paper and stopwatch. This meant we maintained an even distance behind them, trusting or at least hoping they knew what they were doing until I figured out the speed we needed. Since we had been travelling at 90 mph for a while, Greg spitting kumquat seeds out the window and the wind spitting them back at him, we had to slow down to 45 for a while, until we settled into a steady 58 mph pace. As we approached the rolling checkpoint Greg and I counted down the final 15 seconds and we crossed it at exactly the proper time. The officials later said we were one second off, but I still don't think so.

The final transit stage ended at the arches at the

edge of San Felipe. We waited around for Andy and Jim to show up, but then decided to go on to the Hotel Missiones and wait there. At the hotel, the driver of the Sprite was thrilled with the help we had given him and wanted to repay us. We had run out of 35 mm film, so they gave us a roll along with their deep appreciation. Andy and Jim made it to the hotel without us having to form a search party, so we jumped in the Sea of Cortez for a quick swim before going into town for a shrimp dinner. At the awards ceremony, once again the official results varied from my computations. I had learned to adjust, being sufficiently confident in my mathematical abilities. By the official results Fritz finished second in class with an average speed of just over 91 mph and ninth overall. And, thanks to Fritz and a wire hanger, the Dino finished fifth overall.

After the ceremony we retired to our tent for the night. It was a balmy night - a pleasant contrast to last year. Actually, this entire race was a pleasant contrast to last year's La Carrera the car ran well, there were no accidents, the weather was beautiful - what more could you want? The next morning we once more hooked up the support vehicle behind the race car and headed home, choosing the scenic route through the mountains to the Tecate border crossing. All in all, another successful outing.

Chapter 9

Let It Snow, Let It Snow, But Not During a Race

The following year brought with it another La Carrera Classic. Our friend Rick and his friend Joe came out to the ranch from Ohio before the race, towing his '54 Lincoln four door behind his '67 Merc station wagon. Also, our friend Greg came down from Whittier to give us a hand getting the Lincoln ready.

The race this year was going to be run a bit differently. Due to some hotel booking difficulties in San Felipe, it was decided to run from Ensenada to Valle de la Trinidad, the half way point, and then back to Ensenada. The hill climb to La Bufadora was still to be held on the Friday before the race.

The Wednesday before we were due to leave Fritz, Greg, Rick and Joe went up to Long Beach to visit with racing legend Bill Stroppe. While there, they discussed the days of the original La Carrera Panamericana when Bill was preparing the original road race Lincolns, as well as Bill's current projects at that time. He also gave them each an autographed copy of his biography, "Boss - The Bill Stroppe Story."

Meanwhile I was at home leisurely preparing to leave for the race Friday morning. There was one problem with this theory. Fritz told me at the last minute we were leaving a day early, as soon as Rick's friends arrived in their rental car from LA International Airport. So much for leisurely - I hadn't moved that fast since the time I almost stepped on a rattlesnake. And yes, having to watch for rattlesnakes is one of the facts of life out here. At least the car itself was basically ready. Fritz had already updated the roll bar and installed a five point harness in the Lincoln to accommodate this year's rule changes. He also borrowed one of the five pound bottles of Halon fire retardant out of our '29 Model A roadster pickup and plumbed a driver actuated driver's compartment fire system. In an attempt to compensate for the extra weight, Fritz removed the heater system from under the front seat and installed an aluminum block off plate.

We were ready to go around 1:00 p.m. Rick chose to drive his car into town and load it on the trailer there. The rest of us did a little last minute shopping before heading across the border.

We arrived at Estero Beach around 6:00 that evening. After noticing a lack of race cars in the parking area, we decided to work out our accommodations for the evening. As we were about to drive to the resort office the Lincoln chose not to start. Back in the day when we weren't running a generator, this was not an uncommon occurance, but since we had recently re-installed one, it was a bit of a puzzle. Fritz figured out that the cutout relay spring in the voltage regulator wasn't strong enough to deactivate the points, which drained the battery. He tweaked the spring tension lever and got a quick jump from Rick's Lincoln to ours. And I do mean quick, because when you re jumping from twelve volts to six, it has to be fast, or you have to deal with a whole new set of problems.

We reached the resort office, only to learn they no longer allowed tent camping, but they referred us to a campground just down the road. We were on our way to

Diary of a Racer's Wife

check out the alternative camp site and the pricing there, when the Lincoln decided it only wanted to run on five or six cylinders. Hmm... Between that, the drizzle that was starting, and Rick's misgivings about leaving one of his cars unattended at Estero Beach, since the campground charged extra per vehicle, we decided to all chip in and get a room for the night at Estero. That proved providential, as during the night the drizzle became a downpour. Greg, who figured out that I didn't feel like cooking that night, generously bought us all dinner, and shortly thereafter we retired for the evening.

Friday morning the torrential rains of the night before had temporarily abated, so Fritz hurriedly went to the Lincoln to see what was wrong with it. Almost immediately he detected a vacuum leak and learned that our 200 mile old spark plugs had become carbon fouled. Our new friend Marv drove him to the nearest parts store, where he bought a slightly hotter set of Autolight plugs, as that was what was available. He had to go to another parts store just down the street to get a base gasket for the Holley carburetor. After installing these, he still heard a hissing noise, and finally traced it to a cracked vacuum line at the wiper motor.

Meanwhile, it was my job to put smaller diameter tires on the back of the Lincoln to give it a lower gear ratio for the hill climb. Bless their hearts, men kept trying to help me, but I was still proving myself as woman crew chief in a predominantly male sport. Besides, it's not like it was the first time I'd ever had to change a tire - Fritz firmly believed in using up a tire until the air fell out, so I have definitely changed my share and then some. One time we actually had tires on our trailer rust at Bonneville - not the wheels, the tires, because they were so far into the steel cords.

Fritz finished working his magic under the hood,

and the Lincoln sounded like a race car again. Right about the time he finished, the heavens opened again with brief but intense showers. During the dry spells, people would come out from under cover and mill around the race cars that were beginning to arrive. We were happy to see old friends - Frank with his '55 Lincoln, Darren, with his Bug-Eyed Sprite, who told us he still carried the Pick-A-Part screwdriver Fritz had given him for luck, and Bob with his Buick powered Allard. There were also the ubiquitous Porsches, a couple of Alfas, an AC, a Mercedes, and so on, but I was drawn to the Edsel from Ensenada. I've always loved Edsels for some reason, and this one had been built for off road racing. While the owner made last minute efforts to set it up for this race, it had some major handling issues and was unable to compete.

No one seemed to be sure when the hill climb was supposed to start, although that may have been due to the weather, not organizational issues. A late afternoon time was tentatively set, so during the interim we jumped in our Lincoln to show Rick the course and check for this year's potholes. As we headed for La Bufadora, the sky once more opened up on us, this time adding hail to the mix. I wouldn't have wanted to be in an open car at that point, I assure you. The course wasn't bad - certainly no worse than last year - but the rain and hail continued, so the hill climb had to be cancelled.

The drivers meeting was held around 4:30 in the hotel restaurant. We were told that the race would be held regardless of the weather. Since there was no hill climb to determine the starting order, the race organizers were going to make that decision based on their knowledge of the cars and their performance in past races. The road out of town was supposed to close at 7:00 a.m., so all support vehicles needed to be out of town before then. The race drivers were supposed to be at the usual "parade start" location on Shoreline Blvd. by 9:00 to be staged. And, again as usual, the official start to the race would be at the 10 K marker outside of town. The first speed stage would be run from there to the 90 K marker near Independencia. Drivers then had two kilometers to slow down, stop and have their time recorded. Following the speed stage, there was a brief transit section to the 95 K marker, where the next speed stage would begin, ending at the 121 K marker just outside of Valle de la Trinidad. After the control point, the drivers were to proceed into town for lunch. After lunch, the race was going to be run in the reverse direction, ending up at the 10 Kilometer marker, with a transit stage back into Ensenada.

Eduardo, the race coordinator and all around good guy, also told us that due to the war in the Persian Gulf, economic conditions and the weather, that the field for this year's race was very small - I think there were about 23 of us. But he also said that out of gratitude for the die hard entrants who did show up, and because of his love for the sport, the race would not be cancelled. I seriously doubt they made any money on it that year. After paying the *Federales* to close the road, insurance, and medical personnel, including the air evac helicopter, there couldn't have been anything left.

Following the drivers' meeting, we decided rather than get soaked sleeping in our tents, we would again all chip in and get a room. Even Fritz agreed that paying $12 per person was a small price to pay for staying warm and dry. He didn't think we needed to spend money on dinner, however, so Greg and I used Rick's Coleman stove and made spaghetti in our room, using one small saucepan and one skillet. It was a bit of a challenge, but we worked it out and no one went hungry.

After breakfast the next morning, Greg and I were looking for a way to get ourselves and the kids to Valle de la Trinidad before the road closed, having no support vehicle of our own this year. We had originally thought we had a couple of options, including going down with Jim T, but he hadn't shown up yet, and we had to do a bit a scrambling. We had a few tenuous leads when Lucy, codriver of the Corvette, offered us the use of her Toyota 4 Runner and handed Greg the keys. We thanked her profusely, then continued with our preparations for departure. While Greg was back at our room, I took some provisions to the car and opened the door, only to have the alarm blare across the parking lot. I'd never owned a car new enough to have an alarm, so it just didn't occur to me that this one did. Since Greg had the keys and the disarming device, I had to stand there and wait and smile at people giving me strange looks until he got there. After my kids set it off a few times, I started to get used to it. Greg and I had just about finished emptying out our room when Jim arrived in his dad's International truck with a camper on it. He couldn't get his Lincoln going in time, but said he wanted to come down anyway for support. Greg and I gave the room one more hasty inspection and grabbed my kids. Fritz had already left for the false start, and I was a bit concerned that we wouldn't make it out of town before the road closed. It was now after 8:00, and the road should have been closed over an hour earlier. Even in Mexico, they were bound to close it at some point.

On the way out of the parking lot we saw our friend Bruno, who had intended to bring his Lincoln, but had last minute transmission problems, and his friend Joe. We asked them if they wanted to come with us, so they climbed into the back seat. Joe, who was a very tall man, must have felt like a human pretzel back there, but he didn't complain. Fortunately, we found the road out of town without much difficulty, and then found ourselves in the middle of a convoy of ambulances which were heading out to patrol the course. The police were closing the road behind us, and we were stopped once, but we were in an official looking vehicle, white with "Sonoma Racing Group" lettered on the side, and were allowed to continue with no problem. I'm pretty sure Greg convinced them of our importance and our right to continue onward. Hanging out with him was always entertaining.

We were driving into the mountains when we noticed small patches of snow, courtesy of the previous night's storm. We rounded a bend and found ourselves in a beautiful wonderland - the sage and mesquite all covered in soft, fluffy white powder - it was quite lovely. As we "oohed" and "aahed" our way through the snow, we couldn't help but wonder how the wet and occasionally icy road would affect the racers. But soon we were out of the mountains, and the snow, and dropped down into Valle de la Trinidad.

We didn't have long to wait before the first race cars began to appear. First was a 914 Porsche, followed closely by the Pantera. A few others crossed, including Bob's Allard and Charlie and Lucy's Corvette. Around seventh I heard a familiar roar and saw a flash of yellow and black. I yelled, "That's my husband and I'm proud of him!" Okay, it wasn't exactly Shakespeare, but it's what I said at the moment. Rick's car came flying in about a minute later.

Due to snow, the road from Ensenada to Tecate had been closed, with the traffic being rerouted onto the race course. This was naturally going to precipitate cancelling the final two legs of the race. Such is life. As for Fritz, at the false start of the race, an English film crew wanted to take photos of the two road race Lincolns together, so Rick got permission to start 12th, right behind Fritz, instead of 13th, his official position. After the previous night's storm, some of the streets the racers were to take out of town were covered in mud, which only served to obscure the enormous potholes lying in wait for the unsuspecting. The Lincoln had sufficiently heavy duty suspension to survive, but the AC was not as fortunate - some of the potholes it hit were so severe that the front motor mounts broke, rendering it unable to compete.

Once past the treacherous potholes, Fritz had reached the 10 K marker and the "official" start of the race. The first leg was full of surprises. The first revelation was that the Lincoln would not run over 105 mph. Poor Fritz was so frustrated - he could stay right on the tail of a little pink Alfa in the turns, but it would pull away from him in every straightaway. His second surprise was when he met an oncoming sedan - not quite as exciting as the hay truck a few years earlier, but it had the potential to be. In places, Fritz was making use of the whole road trying to save some time. There was yet more excitement provided by the wet roads. Just when he had become accustomed to driving through water, he hit a patch of ice that got his attention. Soon after, Fritz noticed the fuel pressure gauge steadily dropping, along with the car's already limited performance. Fritz saw the Trans Am pulled over on the side of the road, so he pulled in behind them. After learning they had blown their engine, he spent what seemed an eternity looking for a screwdriver. He finally located one of our handy dandy Pick-A-Part screwdrivers and took the fuel filter apart, throwing away the element before putting it back together. This seemed to help the problem somewhat, but the car still wouldn't exceed 105 mph.

At the mandatory stop between stages, Fritz borrowed a wrench from Rick so he could clean the fuel filter at the carburetor, then readjusted the ignition timing. Rick had been having some issues of his own - his Lincoln's transmission wasn't shifting properly. When it was Fritz's turn to leave for the second stage, our Lincoln's speed climbed steadily to 130, and that leg, while short and sweet, passed without incident.

It wasn't all a bowl of cherries for the other competitors either. A green 911 Porsche crashed shortly after the beginning of the race, totaling the car, but fortunately the driver and co-driver were okay. Charlie and Lucy's Corvette blew a head gasket, but it somehow managed to heal itself. Our friend Frank's starter gave up on him at the beginning of the second stage, and he had to be towed to Valle de la Trinidad. Poor Frank - he hadn't been able to finish the race last year either.

We stood around and chatted and waited for the promised lunch that never arrived. The American coordinator compensated for this by buying the racers several of cases of beer for lunch instead. Well, it seemed like a good idea at the time.

Meanwhile, Fritz was helping Frank and his co-driver remove their starter. A local woman named Lupe, another master at making something from nothing, helped them procure enough parts for Fritz to rebuild the starter. She told Fritz he should move to Valle de la Trinidad and go into business with her.

Most of the other racers were gone by the time we had finished with Frank's car and were ready to head back. The kids and I rode in our Lincoln with Fritz, with Rick and Joe following us and Greg and Jim bringing up the rear in the other vehicles. Even though the race was officially over, we didn't exactly obey the speed limit as we headed back to town. Rick seemed to enjoy roaring past the *Federales*, who were still positioned on the side of the road, waving at us, urging us to go faster.

Once we reached Estero Beach, Frank generously gave us approximately 30 gallons of racing gas, complete with octane booster, out of gratitude for Fritz's help with the starter. This was very providential, as there had been a misunderstanding with Jim regarding the gas we had left with him to bring down for the team. Jim made it, but the gas didn't. Oh well, it all works out in the end.

At the awards ceremony that night at the convention center, there were complimentary sodas, beer and sandwiches. Our conjecture was that they were the sandwiches we didn't get for lunch. The overall winner was a highly modified Porsche 914. Rick beat us by 40 seconds, making him the fastest car in our class and 10th overall, with Fritz finishing 11th, with an average speed of 80.2 mph. It had been real, it had been fun, but with the car performing the way it did, it wasn't real fun. One must view these things philosophically, I suppose - there is always another race.

Since the La Carrera Classic was held in March, this was just the beginning of the racing season for us. The first El Mirage of the season would be held in May, and Bonneville in August was just around the corner. Throw in the Antique Nationals, and we had another full year ahead.

As I've previously mentioned, Zeke spent most of his time in Santa Cruz with his mom. While we frequently drove up to see him, there were times when we would fly him down to either San Diego or Ontario airport, which ever had the best deal. On one particular occasion, since Zeke was flying into Ontario, Fritz decided to pick up some junk yard gas while he was in the area. He loaded about 90 gallons worth of containers into the station wagon. We nicknamed it the "Wagon Queen Family Truckster" in honor of the movie "Vacation." "Vacation" was definitely a family favorite, especially since our family vacations bore a strong resemblance in many ways.

Uncharacteristically for Fritz, he left early enough to get gas before Zeke's flight arrived. Since Zeke was only nine or so, his dad went into the airport to pick him up at the gate. When they came out of the terminal into the parking lot, part of the lot had been cordoned off with yellow caution tape, including the area where the Truckster was parked. They stood there for a bit, milling around with the policemen, firemen, and other travelers, trying to figure out what was happening. Since there didn't seem to be any real activity, he finally asked if he could get his car and go home. When the officer asked which car, he pointed to the '72 Ford station wagon. They looked at him incredulously and asked, "That's your car?" This was around the time of Desert Storm, and even back then tensions were running high. Some well-meaning citizen had noticed the car with all of the gas cans, and thought a terrorist was planning to blow up the airport.

Various agencies who weren't already there were called, trying to figure out if what he was doing was legal. One by one, they couldn't find any law against it. Finally, the fire department said one of the containers was not an approved gasoline container and told him he had to get rid of it. As the wagon's tank was full, he offered it to them, and the police, and the highway patrol, and anyone else in range, but no one wanted it. Fritz couldn't just leave it in the parking lot, as that would not have been well received either. At last he was able to leave in in the airport maintenance department for a friend who worked there, and he and Zeke were able to come home. Even between races, there was never a dull moment in our household.

At the June El Mirage we had an unexpected guest. When we arrived at the lake bed, a mouse jumped out of the frame of the station wagon, looking extremely confused. It looked around and decided a dry lake was not a hospitable place, so it jumped back up into the frame. We tore a slice of bread into small pieces and provided a milk jug cap filled with water since its normal sources of nourishment were unavailable. Our family joked about having a 'Full House Mouse' with us, naming it Ralph after the character in the children's book. It isn't that I'm a huge rodent fan, but both Fritz and I felt compassion for the poor little creature and did what we could to help. As far as we knew, Ralph made it back home after the races the next day. After that, it was on its own, since my cats have always been extremely efficient hunters.

It was during this year's Bonneville, though, that I learned about the generosity of some of our fellow racers, and my faith in humanity was restored. Let me preface this by saying that after living in a bad neighborhood in San Bernardino I never kept money in my purse. When someone referred to the Drug King you weren't sure if they were referring to the pharmacy on the corner or the local dealer. For some unknown reason, though, I put every dollar of our money for the week in my wallet. Granted, this was only $250. It was five $50 bills, and it was all we had, but with careful management it would get us through the week and back home. We had stopped to put gas in the '72 Ford station wagon at Ash Springs. We didn't actually buy gas there, just put in some of the junkyard gas that we had brought with us. We went inside and bought a few supplies, and while I was putting the green grapes into the cooler in the back of the car, I set my wallet on the roof of the car, and completely forgot about it. In my defense, I was fairly sleep deprived, and traveling with Fritz and the kids always had an element of chaos and confusion.

It wasn't until we hit Ely, 120 miles later, that I realized what I had done. I was devastated. I could have made all of the excuses I wanted, but the bottom line was it was completely my fault. Fritz, although annoyed, wasn't about to go back and look for it, and said we would borrow money for the week once we were there. So, we pressed on, with zero money, but more than enough gas to reach the salt. Fortunately, Fritz had a couple of generous friends, at least one of whom just opened his wallet and said, "Sure, how much?" Thanks to Rudy, we were able to race that week and feed our children. We weren't able to get the record back we had lost to a Triumph the year before, but we gave it a good try anyway.

On the way home, we stopped again at Ash Springs and asked if by chance anyone had found a wallet. To our surprise, the answer was yes, and we were told where we could go in the little town of Alamo to identify it. When we got there, I was asked to identify it and how much money had been in it, which I did. To our amazement and delight, all $250 was in it, giving us enough money to pay Rudy back for his generous loan. My license was missing, but I figured that having to go to DMV to get another one was a small price to pay.

We were all very tired after our adventures on the salt that week, so we pulled off the freeway into a dirt lot near Yermo, California for a few hours of sleep. We were awakened the next morning not only by the sun streaming through the station wagon windows, but also by the sound of a highway patrol plane that kept circling over us. That seemed a bit peculiar to us at first, but taking a look around, we decided we might perhaps appear the tiniest bit unusual. We were driving our 20-year-old light brown station wagon with wood grain sides with several rows of five-gallon jeep cans tied to the luggage rack on top. The car was surrounded by all of the camping stuff, tools, and other race related paraphernalia we had to remove from the interior so we could sleep in the back. The trailer was a somewhat primitive wooden platform on a single axle. It had a vintage Harley tied to it, which might have seemed slightly incongruous to anyone who didn't know us. Our family looked like we hadn't showered in a week - oh, wait, we hadn't. In spite of liberal use of sunscreen, we were all so sunburned passing airliners probably wondered about the red glow emanating from us. And even though we had done a preliminary cleaning of the car, bike and trailer to remove most of the highly corrosive salt, the occasional big clump would still fall, glaringly white on the sandy brown soil. So, in retrospect, I don't think I can blame him too much for wanting to have a closer look. Who knows, maybe he was just trying to figure out how there could be what appeared to be snow in the middle of the desert in August.

After repacking everything, we decided to take the kids to Calico Ghost Town, now that we had a little money available. We had stopped at Calico on the way home from Bonneville in previous years, and at the time it was a fun and inexpensive side trip to reward the kids for being so good during Speed Week. As we went to pull out the free-way to head toward the Calico exit, there were five Highway Patrol cars there. We wondered if they were waiting for us after being buzzed by the plane multiple times, and sure enough one of them hit the lights and pulled us over, another joined him, pulling in front of us, and the other three just kind of hung out. In all honesty, I'd never been pulled over by five cars and an airplane before, nor have I been since. They wondered about the motorcycle and the gas cans. Most of the cans were empty by this time, so they didn't really have much to say about them.

One of the officers finally said he pulled us over because our brake light on the trailer didn't work. This wasn't particularly shocking since Fritz didn't have it wired, but he acted surprised and went back to check on the connections. Before he went to the trailer he whis-pered to me that when he said, "Try it now," to pull the light switch out one click so the tail light would come on, as it actually worked. So, sure enough, when he called out, "Try that!" that is what I did, even though I would have preferred him to just attach the correct wire. This procedure satisfied the officer, who probably thought it didn't look very bright because of the brilliant desert sunlight shining on it. He did write us a ticket for three-and-a-half-year-old Jason not being in a car seat. Luckily for me, the law at the time was four-years-old or forty pounds, and Jason was close enough to the weight limit that we didn't have to pay the fine.

A day or so after we got home I got a telephone call at around 7:00 in the morning from a Nevada State Trooper. After he identified himself, I was thinking, "Oh no, what did I do wrong in Nevada?" He told me a highway worker had found my license and he wanted to verify my address to send it to me. Like I said earlier, this trip restored my faith in humanity.

Chapter 10

The Earth Is Shifting, Why Won't the Transmission?

After a comparatively uneventful winter, we were ready to go racing again, this time at El Mirage. We were loading the station wagon with supplies for the June 1992 meet, when I went into labor with Christopher. At least we had already settled on a name this time - Fritz wanted to name him after motorcycle racing legend Chris Carr, and as I liked the whole Christian connotation of the name, I agreed. Fritz kept trying to convince me that if I delivered my baby up at the lakes, I would rate the front page of the Bonneville Racing News, but I finally prevailed and got him to take me to the hospital in Escondido, towing the Model A roadster pickup behind the '72 Ford wagon. A friend of ours was following in his van, which was carrying the K Model Harley that Fritz raced. I liked Palomar Hospital better than the one in Fallbrook for a couple of reasons, one of them being I would deliver the baby in my room, and not in the hall.

While I was in the final, really nasty stage of labor, Fritz was standing next to me watching "Memphis Belle" on television. He'd never seen it before, and was mesmerized by it due to his lifelong love of World War II aircraft, more affectionately known as "Warbirds." He was hard of hearing and kept asking, "What did they say, what did they say?" while I was having intense contractions, one right after another.

With all the grace, love and compassion I had, I put my hands on his shoulders, maybe they were closer to his neck, looked him straight in the eye and shouted, "I DON'T CARE WHAT THEY SAID!" He didn't find that helpful, and continued to watch the movie, still trying to hear from the speaker on my bed.

Chris was born around 8:50 Saturday night. As a side note, interestingly enough, Chris has in the last few years had a couple of opportunities to fly in a B-17, like the one in the "Memphis Belle." Destiny? Once he was sure the baby and I were okay, and the movie had ended, Fritz decided to go ahead and go to El Mirage that night, even though I was being discharged the next day. I had to get our friend Jim to take Chris and me home Sunday noon, as Fritz was busy racing. He did set another record with the Harley. The nurses would look at me, Chris and Jim on our way out of the hospital and say to him, "Oh, you must be so proud," etc. - I just smiled and didn't even try to explain. Fritz never did understand why I was angry with him for going to El Mirage. He even wrote, "It's a boy! And another record!" on the side of the station wagon with shoe polish. Apparently, I told him he could go. After 11 hours of labor I probably would have told him anything, but I still couldn't believe he went! It took me about three years to get completely over that one. Well, mostly over it.

A few weeks later it was time to head down to Mexico for the La Carrera Classic. Yes, I was completely out of my mind taking a newborn baby to Mexico. The previous fall, the Lincoln, which had served us faithfully and well for many miles and many races, began having transmission issues. When the problem initially developed, third and fourth gears would not engage early in the drive, but after a bit would start shifting and work fine for the rest of the day. After a few weeks, though, it quit shifting into the higher gears all together, and then we lost first, second, and reverse. We let the car sit over the winter, starting it periodically to keep the engine happy, but figured we had plenty of time to correct the transmission problem before the next race.

Spring came before we knew it. In early June, Fritz figured we had to put everything else on hold, except El Mirage, of course, and work on the Lincoln. We thought we had the problem figured out - after pulling the transmission out, Fritz had found a faulty locking plate nut which holds the torus together. This nut had backed off, and when the torus can't hold pressure, the transmission can't shift. He couldn't find a replacement, so he made one from some 16-gauge steel he had. He reinstalled the transmission on Tuesday, June 23rd, with our plan being to leave on Thursday the 25th. The new locking plate solved the problem with first and second gears, however, the original problem with third and fourth still existed. Since I had just had a baby, and it was inadvisable for me to help pull the transmission this time, on Wednesday our eleven-year-old son Zeke helped his dad. Once the transmission was again out of the car, Fritz spoke with his friend Moe, the hyrda-matic expert in Escondido, about 35 miles from us. After disassembling it in part to check it out, Fritz loaded it into the back of the '56 Ford pickup and drove it down to Moe's shop, where they decided there was a blown seal in the third and fourth clutch pack. As I said before, no pressure, no shifting. There wasn't time to finish it there, so Fritz brought it home to give it a thorough cleaning.

Thursday, the day we were supposed to leave, was spent instead down at Moe's rebuilding the transmission. Our other problem was that our support crew, which had started out as quite a group, had dwindled into me and the kids, including three-week-old Chris. By Thursday night the transmission was back in and working in all gears, but the engine was falling on its face. We decided to call it a night, before it became morning again, and try once more after a few hours of sleep. Fritz cleaned and installed a different carburetor he wanted to try, a 780 cfm Holley, checked the points and cleaned and rearranged the spark plugs, an exercise I like to call 'musical spark plugs'. By 1:30 the car was running well enough for us to head to the border. We hadn't had time to go to Pick-A-Part to get gas for the trip, so decided to use our GMC Caballero for the support vehicle, as it got the best mileage. For those of you unfamiliar with it, the Caballero was the GMC version of the El Camino. I used to call ours the 'El Camangled'.

We had decided that in order to save time we would 'divide and conquer' - Fritz, Zeke and Andy would go to the liquor store for milk; Jason, Chris and I would go to the bank and take out what little money we had. We would then meet at the auto parts store across the street from the bank. I sat and waited in the parking lot for about ten minutes before deciding to go in search of Fritz and my other boys. I found them parked across the street from the liquor store with a dead battery. I took Fritz to a nearby friend's house to borrow his jumper cables, returned to the Lincoln, and carefully jumped the six volt battery in it with the twelve volt battery in the GMC. We then proceeded to the local battery shop where the Lincoln's battery was pronounced mortally wounded. We couldn't really afford $53.00 for a new 6 volt battery, but we were able to purchase a used one for $15.00. What a difference a hot battery makes! We still had to get a new set of plugs, so we returned to the auto parts store to get that handled, then returned the jumper cables to our friend. By this point I decided to get some groceries to feed my hungry children while Fritz installed the new spark plugs.

Around 4:30, a day later and several dollars shorter than planned, we were finally on our way. We stopped by Moe's to thank him again for his help. Before we headed back down the freeway towards the border, I asked Fritz where he wanted to get off I-15. He said we would take 805 to the San Ysidro border crossing. We drove down the freeway with me in the lead. At the north end of San Diego, the freeway splits - I-15 continues south, and Hwy 163 veers off to the right. I was in the far right lane of what would continue to be the 15, and he was in what would become the far left lane of the 163. Simultaneously we realized we were about to be on separate freeways, so also simultaneously, we changed freeways at the last minute, now putting him on the 15 and me on the 163. The problem of course, was figuring out how to find each other - this is before cell phones were common, and even if we had them, he wouldn't have been able to hear anyway. I wasn't particularly amused by the situation, but figured he would go to the same gas station near the border that he always went to, so I headed there. This turned out to be the appropriate choice, and we were once more reunited. The Lincoln's carburetor, however, was flooding and using excessive amounts of gas - six miles to the gallon isn't exactly what you would call fuel efficient. So, while we were stopped, Fritz removed the big Holley and replaced it with our old reliable 600 cfm Holley, which he had brought, thinking it might be needed.

We crossed the border, the Lincoln now running beautifully. Since we were running late, we took the toll road. We normally bypassed it to save the toll fees -$2.30 per car at three stops. $13.80 later, we arrived in Ensenada. The race headquarters was no longer at Estero Beach

119

as in previous years, so our next challenge was to find
the Hotel Villa Corona downtown. It took a bit of driving
around, but we eventually found it. We had missed the
day's hill climb, but at least we arrived in time for the
drivers' meeting.

Other than to note a few corrections to the route
book, the sole purpose of the drivers' meeting seemed to
be to confuse the drivers and navigators. But, it's not the
first time we had ever felt that way, so things seemed to
be settling into as normal a pattern for us as they ever
got. After the meeting we took care of our entry, then
went to a cabin we had reserved on the beach at edge of
town for a good night's sleep. I was crazy enough to take a
three-week-old baby racing in Mexico, but I wasn't crazy
enough to go camping with one in the process. Besides,
even we could afford $28.00 for the night.

The next morning was race day. Fritz checked the
vital fluids in both cars, added a half quart of transmission fluid to the Lincoln as the front seal had developed
a slight drip, but at this point it wasn't anything to be
concerned over. The kids and I headed for the San Felipe highway, and Fritz headed for the Pemex station for
some fuel. On the way to the "false start" downtown, the
Lincoln's engine started missing on one cylinder again, so
while he was waiting for his turn Fritz once more played
the game of 'musical spark plugs' at which he was so
proficient. This produced the desired result - a smooth
running, healthy sounding engine.

Since we had missed the hill climb the previous day,
Fritz had to start near the back of the pack, which was
still notably smaller than in earlier years. Besides Fritz
and another Lincoln, there was a Henry J, a bug-eyed
Sprite, the ubiquitous Porsches, a couple of Alfa Romeos,
an XJX Jag, a Ghia, a Mustang, a Mazda and a couple of
others that I've probably forgotten. This year there was

also a 'fast touring' class for cars without roll bars and other safety requirements, which were only allowed to leave after the 'real' race cars.

Fritz left the false start downtown and headed toward the official start immediately after the other Lincoln, which had some navigational problems. They had missed the second turn. He considered chasing them down, but decided they would be able to work it out without too much difficulty. They arrived at the 10 K marker a few minutes after Fritz, remarking that they hoped the rest of the race would go better. Loyal, the American coordinator for the race who was familiar with Fritz's racing style, asked Fritz to let them round the first turn before he passed them.

When Fritz left the starting line, the Lincoln was running flawlessly. By the second turn he passed the other Lincoln. This isn't actually quite as impressive as it sounds - the driver of the other Lincoln had pulled over, possibly to get some water out of the trunk.

The first speed section through the mountains lasted approximately 17 miles. During one of the straightaways on the other side of the mountains, the Lincoln's speedometer climbed to 130 mph. Fritz had just settled into having some serious racing fun when trouble once more reared its head, this time in the form of the transmission slipping as he rounded a turn. He was slowing down when the transmission, running out of fluid, shifted itself down into second gear. Fritz put it in neutral and pulled over. He removed his helmet and seatbelt, jumped out of the car, opened the trunk, pulled out half of a can of 'Trick Shift' and a long funnel, opened the hood, removed the dipstick, inserted the funnel, poured in the fluid, replaced the dipstick, closed the hood, closed the trunk, threw the funnel behind the back seat, got in the car, got back out of the car, removed the keys from the trunk lock, got back in

the car, refastened his helmet and harness while starting
the engine, and took off. All of this substantially cut into
his average time in the first speed section. I later timed
him as he recreated these actions and the whole procedure took about a minute and a half - it may have taken
me longer to describe it than for him to do it.

After the first speed section, there was a 22-mile-
long transit stage, which was untimed. The racers,
though, felt no compulsion to slow down, except during
a section with some nasty potholes. Fritz was cruising
at about 120 when the tranny again ran out of fluid and
downshifted, this time without warning. I later overheard
him say, "I didn't know that engine would tach 9000 rpm
without blowing up." He again added fluid - about two
quarts this time, and took off.

The next speed section was a flying kilometer, de-
signed to get a top speed on the racers. The cars started
from a dead stop, had one kilometer to get up to speed,
were timed through the second, and had a third kilometer
to slow down and stop. The theory was there was to be a
green flag at the beginning of the timed kilometer and a
checkered flag at the end of it. Other than the fact that
the Lincoln could have used two or three kilometers to
get up to its full speed potential, it started off fine. Fritz
soon saw a man with a checkered flag. Thinking perhaps
he had missed the green flag, he started to slow down, but
the official waved him on. He accelerated again, averaging
109 through the kilometer. He saw another official type
person by the side of the road, but didn't see the flag until
he was passing him there was a folded up green flag half
hidden behind the man's leg. At this point he was unsure
of whether or not that was the end of the speed section, so
he stayed on the throttle for a bit longer. About four miles
after the end of the stage, the Lincoln again ran out of
transmission fluid.

Meanwhile, the kids and I were waiting in the scorching heat at Valle de la Trinidad for the race cars to begin arriving. I used the time to buy a watermelon and put it in the ice chest. The GMC didn't have working air conditioning - Fritz felt a/c used up too much horsepower and disabled it in nearly every vehicle we owned. After about an hour's wait -it only seemed like three or four because of the heat and the kids - the purple 914 Porsche, which had won last year, came speeding down the hill and turned the corner toward the service area used in the previous year. A few minutes later other cars followed down the hill, but instead of turning where the Porsche had, they continued straight toward San Felipe. I figured they would realize their mistake and return shortly, but more cars kept going by, and I began to wonder if it was the Porsche and I that made the mistake. I contemplated going in search of them, but decided to wait and see what Fritz did first - after all, he was the one I was waiting for. And waiting. After about ten minutes, a string of cars came back from the other direction. Apparently there was supposed to be a flagman telling them where to turn, but he didn't materialize. At this point I was seriously starting to wonder about Fritz - it wasn't like him to finish in the back of the pack. I really started to wonder when the sweep vehicles came through and the Federales reopened the road to public traffic. Concerned, I drove down to the service area to ask if anyone knew what became of him. I was in the process of doing so when I saw a familiar tall, bearded figure strolling toward me through the crowd. My panic subsided and the smile returned to my face as he reached me. When I asked him what had happened and where the car was, he responded, "Didn't you see that yellow blur streaking past you?"

Back in the real world, though, he had run out of transmission fluid to put in the car, and had gotten a ride into town in one of the sweep vehicles. The other Lincoln had been experiencing cooling problems, and showed up after the sweep vehicles as well. We drove to the local auto parts store for more fluid, and as we drove the 20 or so miles back to the Lincoln, we discussed the logistics of trying to finish the race or limping back to Ensenada. After a little thought, Fritz said, "Well, we're not dead yet." Somehow this didn't surprise me. We poured in two quarts of fluid and headed toward Valle de la Trinidad.

After about 12 miles, he had to pull over to add more. By the time we reached Valle de la Trinidad, the other racers had already left for the next checkpoint. We added more fluid and Fritz tore off after them, with me and the kids faithfully bringing up the rear. He reached the check point in plenty of time, but by this time we had once more exhausted our supply of transmission fluid and were soliciting donations - transmission fluid, motor oil, anything more viscous than water that we could pour in to keep the Lincoln moving. Fritz had read somewhere that in an emergency, light motor oil could be used in a hydra-matic transmission, and we considered being stuck in the middle of a Mexican desert an emergency. We supplemented our transmission fluid/motor oil concoction with some Kendall Nitro 70 drain oil from a friend's 432 mph streamliner. That may sound a bit odd, but we never left home without it.

After the last of the cars in the fast touring class left, the little entourage of support vehicles, including me in the Caballero, followed them down the highway. I had been cruising along for a while when I crested a hill and saw a set of fresh skid marks about 100 yards long. They ended before they reached the opposite side of the road, but I slowed down anyway to make sure no one had gone into the ditch. At last I reached the end of the race, relieved that I hadn't seen "Old Yeller", as Fritz sometimes called our Lincoln, parked on the side of the road.

When I got there, however, I did notice the Lincoln was parked almost in the driveway of the parking lot, instead of in one of the stalls. Fritz told me that was where it had run out of fluid, and it would go no farther. The engine ran beautifully, but he had been forced to stop several times, including twice during the speed stage, to add fluid. Needless to say, that didn't help his average speed. At this point, though, we felt that simply by finishing we had won.

Remember the long, thick black skid marks I had been concerned about earlier? It turns out those were made by the Lincoln when it had run out of fluid and the rear wheels had locked up.

After chatting a bit with the other racers we decided it was time to go get some gas. There was one problem with this - the Lincoln's transmission wouldn't engage in first, second or reverse gears. At least it was still running, though. The other Lincoln competing had overheating problems, and showed up on the back of its support truck. Fritz took the GMC to the Pemex station and used the end of our money to fill a couple of five-gallon gas cans for the Lincoln. Our friend Jim, bless him, offered to loan us enough money to get back home.

We then decided on our next course of action. I was less than enthusiastic about the prospect of towing the Lincoln using Jim's tow strap and my Caballero. That little V- six got good mileage, but in general was pretty gutless - once going up a steep grade not far from home, Zeke had jumped out to push, and it helped! We decided to try another option first - push the car fast enough to see if the transmission would engage in third gear. Or any other gear, as far as that goes - at this point we weren't fussy. Between Jim, Fritz, Zeke and myself, we were able to push it by hand fast enough for the governor to allow third gear engagement. Andy would have pushed, too, but he had to watch his little brothers while I helped. Fritz was able to take off, with Jim following in his Lincoln convertible and me in the GMC. I expected to find him pulled over somewhere within the next 20 miles or so to add fluid, but it seems the Lincoln didn't lose nearly as much at 55 mph as it did at 105. We made it back to Ensenada with only a couple of stops, and one of those was to help a fellow competitor with a burned out coil in his Bug-eyed Sprite.

The next problem was the plethora of stop signs and traffic signals in Ensenada, since Fritz had no lower gears to work with. He only came to complete stops when absolutely necessary, and had to jump out and push to get the car moving again so he could take off. This method worked pretty well as long as the streets were downhill. The last stoplight, however, was pointing up hill, and required a little nudge from me in the Caballero to get the Lincoln moving. It made me wish I was in our '72 Ford station wagon. Not only was that car as indestructible as a tank, it had enough power to push a Mac truck. If wishes were horses...

We finally reached the Villa Corona Hotel race headquarters, where we relaxed and ate the ice cold watermelon I had bought earlier for a dollar, sharing it with anyone who wanted some. A few hours later it was time for an excellent traditional Mexican dinner, complete with mariachis, and the awards ceremony. Fritz placed 15th overall and third in his class, with an average speed of 68.35 mph. This was not particularly surprising, with the number of stops he had to make during the speed sections. There was only one incident - one of the Porsches in the 'fast touring' class had rolled his car near the end of the race, totaling it. The driver however, was fine and attended the awards ceremony.

After the awards ceremony we decided to head back to the states. Being low on money, we took the inland route home to avoid the expense of the toll road. We drove for an hour or so, with Jim in the lead, then Fritz in our Lincoln, and me bringing up the rear. I was half asleep and didn't want them to see me weaving all over the road in front of them - I would have gotten yelled at, but would have had to keep going anyway.

We finally pulled over for the night to sleep in our cars at a place Fritz called the 'Halfway House', since it is halfway between Ensenada and Tijuana. When we woke up early the next morning, Jim asked if we had felt the earthquake an hour or so earlier. Fritz and I both responded, "What earthquake?" Fritz thought Jim was just playing a joke on us by shaking the car, and I was so exhausted that I hadn't felt a thing. We learned a bit later that Southern California had experienced a 7.4 quake, which is a pretty good shaker by any standard. Maybe it was the quake, maybe it was the fact that it had cooled down and the fluid was more viscous, maybe it was just God's way of being nice to us, but for some reason, the Lincoln's transmission again had low gear until we reached the U. S. border.

Once back in California, it stopped working again, and this posed a new set of challenges. Since we had to drive on the freeway, I used the Caballero to push him up to 20 mph or so when third gear would engage and he could take off. We had to stop for gas at one point, so I had to tow him both to the gas station and back up to the freeway with the tow strap, where I would get behind him and push him up to speed. Two of San Diego's finest pulled us over when they saw me towing him up the entrance ramp to the freeway, explaining to us that towing like that wasn't allowed on the freeway. Fritz explained what we were doing, and while the younger cop was a bit dubious, the older of the two thought it sounded reasonable, and we were allowed to proceed.

We stopped at the San Diego Roadster Club picnic on the way home, and spent a good portion of the day there. That was something we always enjoyed as a family, but I admit I would have enjoyed it more if I hadn't been so worn out from Mexico. We finally headed back home toward the ranch. I stuck to Fritz like superglue so I could push the Lincoln at traffic signals. When we finally reached home, I practically kissed the dirt, saying, "Of all the places we go, I like home the best." I understood how Dorothy felt in the Wizard of Oz - too bad I didn't have any ruby slippers!

A couple of months later it was time for Bonneville again. I contemplated the sanity and safety of taking a two-month-old baby to the salt, and decided that I could keep him cool, shaded and hydrated, and ignored the sanity part of the equation. I know that some people there thought I was irresponsible to take Chris, but I was breast feeding, and Fritz wanted me to go, so we went. We ran the K Model, as usual. Tiny Christopher was fine, although he had a couple of cranky moments. I couldn't blame him, but I know a number of adults who have cranky moments at Bonneville, too. Chris has since told me he was glad I took him, because not many people can say they went to Bonneville at the age of two months. And, in general, he did well, which is better than we did with the bike. It wasn't awful, it just wasn't great. All in all, it wasn't a particularly eventful Speed Week, but Mexico had been eventful enough to last me for a little while.

Chapter 11

Water, Water Everywhere, But Not in My Radiator

After the transmission problems with the Lincoln in the previous La Carrera Classic, Fritz and I decided that we weren't going to wait until the last minute to get ready for the '93 race, which was scheduled for May 21-22. The expression "life is what happens to you while you're busy making other plans" was very applicable in this case. Between our other racing endeavors, a major flood ripping through our canyon destroying roads, bridges, and making daily survival a real effort, raising four kids, etc., the Lincoln was set aside.

The January flood itself was quite the experience. I had paid $35 each for two tickets to the SCTA banquet, and I was going to go come hell or high water. We left during the worst storm of that particular decade, barely making it out of the canyon before the roads were all completely flooded. We spent a couple of days after the banquet in La Habra Heights with Dick and Sally while the rain continued to fall. Eventually it let up, so we decided to see if we could make it home. All telephone communication with our neighbors was non-existent. We had to take back roads, with Fritz getting out a couple of times to wade through water crossings to literally make sure the road was still there. We made it to within a few miles of our house before the poor little GMC Caballero we were driving became mired in the mud and would go no further. This had been a paved road, but you really couldn't tell that anymore. By this time it was dark, but we decided to hike home and cross our creek using the neighbor's suspension bridge. When we got back down to De Luz Road from where we were stuck, we had to navigate a water crossing that didn't normally exist. Not wanting to take any chances, Fritz helped Andy through the stream, and then returned twice to carry Jason and finally seven-month-old Chris. We made it to the neighbors' driveway, only to find that the bridge we would have used to walk over De Luz creek, now a raging river, had washed away, leaving us stranded on the wrong side. We walked down to the remains of our driveway, which had been washed out by the normally small seasonal creek that runs parallel to it, and went to another neighbor's house, waking them up and asking for shelter for the night, which they graciously provided.

In the morning we took a look at our creek, which was roughly 150 feet wide at our crossing and around eight or ten feet deep, and running fast. We were concerned for our elderly neighbor and our animals which he was caring for, so when we heard a news helicopter land up in the hills behind us, the neighbor who had given us shelter took us up there to chase it down. Without much difficulty, we were able to convince them to fly us over the creek onto a flat area adjoining our property so we could check on Ray and get to our cabin. They got a story and I got my first helicopter ride. We got home to no phone and no power, but our neighbor and our animals were all okay, which was of course the important thing. The phone and power outage both lasted about a week. After a day or two of dry weather, Fritz was able to wade/ swim back across the creek and find someone to help get the Caballero unstuck, although we had to wait for the creek to go down and then rebuild our driveway before we could actually drive it up to the house.

Having a car didn't matter too much at that point, though, because the paved crossing of the Santa Margarita River completely washed away, as had most of the other crossings between us and the outside world. There really wasn't anywhere to go. The Red Cross flew food and necessities into the fire station half-mile up the road from us for the first several days, until a temporary bridge could be built at one of the smaller crossings. It looked like it had been built from a giant 'erector set', but it worked. One of the local news stations interviewed Fritz, who was very good at that sort of thing. He could make getting a hangnail seem dramatic if he had an audience. It was six months before a permanent bridge was built over the Santa Margarita, allowing us to make a normal 15 to 20 minute drive into town, instead of nearly an hour each way. The school district reopened the little one room school house about two miles up the road from us for the kids who couldn't get into town, and 11-year-old Andy got to ride his motorcycle, a 75cc Honda, to school most days. All in all, it was quite the adventure, but it did make survival rather time consuming.

Nothing could stop us from making it to El Mirage, however. Over the winter, before the flood, I had acquired a '49 Ford business coupe from some friends who used to race it at El Mirage and Bonneville. Some people called it pink, some called it orange; I just called it my chance to play too. It had belonged to another woman racer, and painted on the trunk are the words "Hell, no, it's not my husband's car!" Fritz rebuilt the engine that came with it, a screaming 300 cubic inch flathead V-8. We headed to the lakes in May with the '49 in tow as well as the Harley. I'll never forget my first pass down the lake bed. I admit to

131

being nervous. It wasn't because racing is dangerous - I know that, but you can't dwell on it or it will either bite you or you will be ineffective. It was because I am a female, and even though there are other women who race, it is a predominantly male sport, and I wanted to uphold my gender's honor. Even in later years driving a rock truck on construction jobs, I felt I had to work twice as hard as any man to gain the same amount of respect.

After leaving the starting line, fear was forgotten and I was just trying to keep it more or less straight - my steering box was a bit on the worn side, and the car tended to wander a bit. Fritz told me that having a loose steering box was good practice and that it would make me a better driver. In retrospect, he was probably correct. Over the course of my life I have had to deal with some, shall we say, interesting driving experiences, and I was probably better equipped due to my time driving with a worn out steering box. During my first run I was able to shift smoothly, and keep an eye on the tach, and before I knew it I was through the timing lights and pulling over to the return road. My first pass was only 102 or so, but it did feel really good to be in that car in that place at that speed, although I admit a certain relief when it was over - I hadn't done anything to screw up. On a later run, as a joke, we installed Chris's car seat on the passenger side, as people knew I had my kids with me wherever I went. Someone did actually ask if I was going to try to take him. I hope he was joking. Another time I strapped a giant stuffed bunny into the passenger seat before heading down the course. Why I had a giant stuffed bunny at El Mirage was the real question, however.

With the May El Mirage behind us, it was time to focus on the La Carrera Classic. We decided to make it a team effort this year. Let's face it, after eight years of being pit crew/crew chief, I was ready to play too. Fritz wore himself ragged between working on the Lincoln transmission, the '49, and trying to make enough money to keep us from starving. Complications developed while he was working on the Lincoln's hydra-matic, and with work still needing to be done to my Ford, something had to give. Since Tom from Pick-A-Part had already agreed to sponsor my car, we decided to focus on it. Also, my sister Sally had agreed to be my navigator and had arranged for the time off work, and we didn't want to disappoint her.

This year's choice of support vehicle was Sally and Dick's Suburban. While Fritz was getting his tools together for the trip, he looked over at the Lincoln, sitting on its jack stands, shook his head in disgust and said, "I can't believe Dick and I are going to Mexico to be pit crew for a couple of girls!"

We arrived in Ensenada late in the evening, sorry that we were not able to make the hill climb that afternoon, but relieved to be there at all. For the first time since we had been running this race, we were stopped going into Mexico and questioned about taking the '49 into the country. Between the border official's broken English and our broken Spanish, and a half an hour of time, we eventually got the matter straightened out. We never did figure out why they had stopped us. At the hotel we took care of entry details, with the exception of tech inspection. New that year was the requirement for both driver and co-driver to purchase for $100 a Mexican Rally Federation competition license if not in possession of an SCCA or other FIA affiliate license for insurance purposes. Luckily for me, I had just run my '49 Ford at El Mirage, and had an SCTA competition license that sufficed. That meant we only had to come up with the extra money for Sally. It was one of those situations where I was glad Fritz was able to talk people into things, because we couldn't afford another $100.00 if they hadn't accepted my SCTA license.

Diary of a Racer's Wife

Early the next morning we returned to race headquarters from our $28 beach bungalow. The Hotel Coro-
na, race headquarters, wanted $81, which was a bit too
expensive. It was our first real chance to see the competition. We were somewhat disappointed with the lack of
vintage entries -my '49 was the oldest car there, and the
only flathead. There were a couple of Lincolns, a '54 Corvette, and the usual assortment of Porsches, bringing the
vintage field up to around eight, including me. All together there were about 30 entries and a handful of cars that
didn't meet the tech requirements which were allowed to
run behind the main pack in the "fast touring" class.

Another new requirement for this year was a mini
physical where the medics checked heart rate, blood
pressure and blood type. So, after getting the car through
technical inspection, and Sally and I checked, I gave Fritz
and Andy last minute instructions about our 11-month-
old baby Chris. This accomplished, Sally and I got ready
for our departure.

The '93 race was to run from Ensenada about 70
miles to Valle de la Trinidad and back to Ensenada on
Highway 3. The parade start of the race was directly in
front of the Hotel Corona on the beach side of Shoreline
Boulevard. Fritz told me to go down the street, make a
U-turn and come back to stage for the start. I followed a
line of racers, including a couple of Lincolns and a little
yellow Porsche, who were following a police car. When
they went down several more blocks and turned left, I
thought perhaps they were making a big loop back to the
starting line to give the spectators a thrill. By the time
I decided they were headed out of town, I was afraid if I
turned around I would get hopelessly lost in the labyrinth
of Ensenada's streets - I'd done that before, and didn't
really care to repeat it. So, I ended up following the others
out of town to the official start of the race, annoying the

heck out of my husband for not just listening to him to begin with. After all, he had done this a number of times, had been racing since the invention of the wheel, to hear him talk, and I knew it would be years before he would let me live it down. Of course, this led to my repeated assurances that in the future I would always listen to him and do exactly as he said. Unless, of course, he was wrong.

At the time, though, I had other problems. The engine in the '49 coupe looked and ran great, but it was based on what we knew to be a cracked block. It had so many cracks you could practically see through it. We didn't have time to put another engine together for the car before the race, and had done as much testing as time permitted. We had added some block sealer and I had run the car successfully at El Mirage the week before, top speed 108, and at that time it looked like the sealer might hold. Running through down town Ensenada and climbing the grade out of town, though, I learned the cold hard facts. Actually, "cold" is a poor choice of words, as I watched the temperature gauge climb and was forced to pull over to cool down the engine. Compression from the combustion chamber on number five cylinder was leaking into the cooling system and pushing water out the radiator's overflow tube. I poured most of the two-and-a-half gallons of water I had in the trunk into the radiator and proceeded to the official start at the 12 K marker, only to overheat again. After scrounging more water and staging the car, it was at last my turn to be counted down and we were officially on our way.

Before the race I had to continually reassure Fritz and Sally that I wouldn't drive over my head, which meant too fast to react to the conditions. As he reminded me, to finish first you must first finish. With my over-heating issues, I was happy just to start. While driving, though, several conditions manifested themselves which made it obvious that I would have to take it somewhat easy. First was the 'hard spot' in the steering box, which made mountain driving an interesting experience, to say the least. Another way to put that would be 'pretty darned scary'. Second was a problem with my manual T-10 transmission, which didn't like to stay in third gear when eased up on the throttle. My fix for this was to have poor Sally hold the shifter in third when I needed both hands, which, through the mountains, was frequently. And then, of course, there was the cooling issue. I tried a variety of speeds and techniques, but the results were always the same - the needle on the temperature gauge would inexorably creep up to 220, and I would have to pull over and add water to cool it down.

My other problem was my brakes weren't exactly as responsive as I would have liked them to be. I went to pull over at a wide spot on the road for water, and I may have been coming in a bit faster than I thought I was. With a ditch gaping in front of us, a couple of cars right next to me, and the rear end of the '49 dancing around on the gravel with the brakes locked up, it was a bit intense for a few seconds. We ended up in the ditch, with the nose pointing toward the road. As the angle was not entirely ideal, I asked Sally to get out of the car while I drove it out, just in case there were complications. It came out easily, though, and I never bothered to tell Fritz about that little episode -I edited my version to where we 'almost' went in the ditch. Okay, so we almost *didn't* go in the ditch -I was only off by one little word. I am not in the habit of bending the truth, but I knew I would never hear the end of it if I told him. From that time on I tried to slow down a bit farther in advance whenever possible.

A pattern soon developed. Cruise for a while, heat up, pull over, wait for Fritz and Dick to bring more water and take off. Between having to wait for water and getting behind a slow semi truck which had inadvertently gotten on the race course, I was soon lagging behind and missed some of the checkpoints. Having had experience a few years earlier in the Pan Am with Mexican semis, I was hesitant to pass him until I knew I could clear him.

Due to the excessive amounts of rain received over the winter, there were a couple of water crossings which had to be negotiated. We were approaching one such crossing behind a "Ferrari Wanabe" and a Bronco type vehicle. The replica had slowed to a crawl through the water, as had the Bronco. Unfortunately, I didn't have the advantage of their power brakes, and while I slowed as much as I could I had to take evasive action. This meant passing the two vehicles through the water, completely drenching the driver of the Bronco. I learned just how wet I'd gotten him when I had to pull over a little while later for water, and he stopped to see if I needed any help. I think my legend grew a bit that day, because he must have told nearly every participant in the race, and I heard him retelling the story later at El Mirage. Naturally I explained and apologized profusely, and he agreed being soaked was preferable to me rear ending him.

Toward the end of the race, we were back in the mountains looking for a place to pull over for water when my temperature gauge, which was showing a toasty 230 degrees, quit working. Upon opening the hood, I found the sending unit had come unsoldered from the heat. Poor car. Fritz told me to stop more frequently since I couldn't tell how hot the engine was getting. I managed to be pretty good about this for a while, but when it came to the last 20-mile stretch I just couldn't help myself and I kept going. There was a cool ocean breeze blowing through the canyon, the car was running beautifully and while I had missed my checkpoints I had a pretty good race going with the replica Ferrari.

At the official end of the race I waited for Fritz and
Dick. When they arrived, I was reprimanded for driving
so far without adding water. Once the race was over it
was as if the car knew it didn't have to try anymore and it
was a challenge to keep it running back to race headquarters. I had to cruise through a couple of stop signs using
the 'slow and go' tactic, but finally made it back to the
Hotel Corona.

As I missed some of the checkpoints I did not receive
an official finishing position, but I had run the entire race
without crashing or completely terrifying my sister. She
didn't know at the time that 4,000 rpm on the tachometer
with my gear ratio meant we were cruising at 104 mph,
which was as fast as I wanted to push it under the circumstances. Unofficially, I finished second in the Turismo
Menor class behind the Mustang and around 20th overall.
On the way home, the immigration officer at the border
crossing saw the car on the trailer and asked if we had
won. When Dick replied, "Not exactly," the officer said,

"Well, you'll just have to go back and try again until
you win. We don't need any more losers in California."
Maybe I didn't win, but I did prevail over adversity with
the help of family, friends and a bit of God's grace, so I
was comfortable with myself at the time.

In the early fall, Fritz was offered a position on the
pit crew for our friend Charlie during the Pan Am scheduled for the end of October. It was very strange having
him go to Mexico without me for a few weeks, but I understood that he felt he had to go. I tried to teach him one
Spanish phrase - *"Yo quiero mi esposa"* - my somewhat
mangled version of "I want my wife," which I told him to
use whenever women threw themselves at him, which
seemed to happen from time to time. He flew into Mexico City and met up with the rest of the crew there before
heading the remainder of the way down to the Guatema-

lan border. There were a few issues he had to deal with on the Henry J, but he was most definitely a brilliant mechanic and extremely inventive when it came to problem solving, which served him - and Charlie - well. All in all, he had a great time down there, but I was very happy when he returned home.

It was somewhere during this time frame that I became secretary for the San Diego Roadster Club, a position which I held for five years. Fritz had been in the Rod Rider Club for years, but had neglected to pay his dues on time the year before, and couldn't rejoin as they had already reached their membership quota. Since club membership was required to race, he joined the SDRC, with me joining the following year after I had a car to play with. I enjoyed being secretary as it was a good opportunity to express my sense of humor while relating the events of the meetings to those not able to attend. It also kept club members who lived out of state in touch with happenings at El Mirage.

I loved El Mirage, but it could be a very unforgiving place. One meet I watched a friend's race car burn to the ground - praise God he was able to get out of it first. In later years, I was waiting at the starting line with my friend Terry. My son Andy had just run on one of the Harleys and I was going to bring them both back to the pits via the return road at the same time. The president of SCTA, who, incidentally, was the same person whose car had burnt to the ground all those years earlier, jumped in the truck and said, "I'm taking this truck. We just had a motorcycle go down."

Thinking it was Andy, I said, "I'm going with you," and firmly planted myself in the passenger seat. It turned out that it was actually the rider that had gone down the track right after Andy. He had been involved in an incident at Muroc a few months before where he had been

139

injured, and there was some question as to whether he was completely healed from that. He came off the bike at around 180 mph this time, and suffered some serious injuries, but eventually recovered.

Not everyone is as fortunate. At another El Mirage meet, I witnessed a friend and fellow club member lose his life when his streamliner went out of control and started rolling and flipping end for end, completely demolishing it. I watched his father and brother and friends struggle with their grief, but eventually build another car and return to racing. I get it -it was just what we did.

My car was REALLY thirsty...

Chapter 12
The Good, the Bad, and the Soggy

      Winter passed with yet another flood. This time I lost my '68 Cougar, the only car I ever really loved. The ground was saturated from recent rains, but it was still possible to wade through the creek, even though the sandy bottom was too soft to drive through without getting stuck. My car, two friends' trucks, and one of our trailers were parked on the far side on the dry sand, but still in the creek bed. During the night it began to rain heavily and a flash flood came through. Fritz and I had been under a lot of stress, and were so exhausted we didn't hear the rain begin - normal procedure was if it started raining hard we'd get up and move the vehicles to higher ground. I got up around 5:30 the next morning and walked down to the creek to see if it was possible to get the kids across to the bus stop. It wasn't. I could still see the reflection of one of my hubcaps from the flashlight I was carrying, but I went back and told Fritz as soon as it was light he needed to move the cars.

      We went down to the creek just after 6:00, but it was already too late. All you could see of my Cougar was the orange Union 76 ball on the end of the antenna and a ripple in the water where it flowed over the body. A log had smashed through the windshield of one of the pickups, and the other one was nowhere in sight. It eventually showed up pretty crunched about a quarter mile downstream. Actually, crunched is a fairly mild description.

The cab was flattened like a pancake, and there wasn't a straight panel left anywhere on the poor thing. The owner of that truck, who was living with us at the time, was pretty irate that we hadn't done something to prevent his loss. It's not like we were exactly thrilled ourselves, but sometimes you just have to accept what exists.

As we stood on the bank, surveying the situation, the trailer we normally towed to Bonneville decided to begin floating down the river. Fritz and I stood on the bank and waved goodbye to it. What else could we do? We did find it a few days later, after the flood subsided enough for us to look for both it and the missing truck. The trailer was about a half mile downstream, so we decided to chain it to a tree until the rainy season was over and we could retrieve it with the jeep, as it wasn't remotely possible under the current conditions. The word 'current' applied in more ways than one. The trailer suffered some damage, but we were able to beat it back into shape. I was amazed by the condition of the license plate. I don't know what kind of plastic and glue the DMV uses on their registration stickers, but it is some good stuff. The plate was definitely a bit crumpled and dinged from its adventures in the river, but the sticker was still absolutely perfect. This flood happened on Valentine's Day, so I called it the St. Valentine's Day Massacre of 1994. Eventually we also got the Cougar out of the creek bed and began the drying out and cleaning process, but it was clear a major restoration was going to be required.

Spring came, and with it the new racing season. Since the Lincoln was conspicuously absent at last year's La Carrera Classic, Fritz was determined not to miss the '94 event. The entry fee had been raised to $640, which included hotel accommodations and the necessary competition licenses for both co-driver and driver. This seemed problematic to me at first, as I've always felt a strange compulsion to pay my bills and feed my children. Trivial details like this never concerned Fritz. If he was determined to go to a race, that was what would happen. Thank goodness Pick-A-Part and the Road Race Lincoln Register came through for us and we had a charge account at the local auto parts store.

Those minor details taken care of, all that was left was to prepare the Lincoln and the '49 for the race. We began this time with the Lincoln's hydra-matic transmission, to assure that the Lincoln would get its turn this year. That actually went smoothly this time, so we decided to try to get the '49 Ford coupe ready to run as well. We borrowed a mild flathead from my brother-in-law Dick, which Fritz had gone through a year earlier. After last year's issues with my cracked block, we felt that while this engine was smaller and less powerful, it should prove more reliable.

So, with a week and a half to go before the race, Dick and Greg came down to our ranch from Whittier for a day to help swap engines in my car. Nothing seems to go right when you are in a hurry, and this, while normally a simple task, was no exception. We finally got almost everything transferred to the new engine - heads, water pumps, distributor, etc., but when it came time to install the clutch and flywheel, we realized the clutch was somewhat burnt and the flywheel needed to be resurfaced. As usual, we were out of time and money simultaneously, so we decided to run what we had, but to replace the shifter with one of Fritz's Hurst competition shifters. He felt it would reduce my excuses for abusing the clutch. He had to modify the linkage, but was able to piece it together out of miscellaneous four speed transmissions he had, so that left us with one remaining item - a water pump belt. We had removed it when I was running the engine as a dry block at El Mirage, and it had disappeared into that abyss

143

where everything goes we put in a "safe place." Since there is no generator or tensioner, the belt had to be the exact length and width we needed. We couldn't come up with one locally, so Fritz decided we would get one on the way to Mexico.

Fritz was test driving the Lincoln when he remembered that he wanted to change to steering box. He went so far as to borrow one, but decided he didn't have time to install it. The Lincoln also developed a water pump leak that seemed to heal itself, and started fouling spark plugs. A new set of plugs fixed this temporarily. Fritz had offered to help this year's organizer of the event, our friend Charlie, in any way possible, so he had to be at headquarters early Thursday. Dick, my co-driver Sally, and my nephew Ryan came down Wednesday evening. For the sake of expediency, we decided Fritz, our son Andy and his friend Matt would go ahead in the Lincoln, and the rest of us, including sons Jason and Chris, would follow in Dick's Suburban, towing the '49. It was our task to pick up a water pump belt, spark plugs, and carburetor cleaner on the way. Fritz figured he would clean the Lincoln's carb in his leisure time down there and solve the plug fouling problem, which had recurred. The only reason I mention this is because it took an eternity to perform this seemingly simple task. I had to explain the numbering system on fan belts to the kid working at the auto parts store, who, bless his heart, had absolutely no clue what I wanted. I hated to tell him how to do his job, but hopefully he learned something from me, and we finally got back on our way.

Meanwhile, Fritz, Andy and Matt were in Ensenada at the Hotel Corona gorging themselves on the complimentary buffet and soaking up what little sun there was, while keeping an eye on an approaching storm. We finally arrived, with water pump belt in hand, after the buffet had ended. Sigh. We had no such luck with the spark plugs -the parts kid had never heard of a Champion H10 or an F11YC before, and cross referencing was not his area of expertise.

The skies were growing ominously darker and other racers were out covering their cars. One of the most notable of the other race cars, to us, anyway, was Ak Miller's famed Caballo de Hierro, or Iron Horse. Fritz had already taken care of the Lincoln, so we unloaded the '49 and got it through tech. The tech inspectors this year were very knowledgeable and thorough, and had a good sense of humor, which is always something I appreciate in a tech inspector. In fact, there have been times in our racing career when the inspector's sense of humor was downright essential, especially at Bonneville.

After a heavy rain Thursday night, the weather was still a bit unsettled Friday morning. After test driving my car, which I hadn't had the opportunity to do since we swapped the engine, I was a little unsettled too. One of the parts we had taken from the larger engine and installed on the smaller one was the intake manifold, complete with three Holley two-barrel carburetors. The problem with this was it was way too much fuel for the smaller engine at low speed, and it kept fouling plugs, changing my healthy V8 into a coughing four cylinder. No big deal, we thought - we were just going to put smaller jets in the carburetors. We reached for the 35 mm film containers we'd brought, expecting to find them full of Holley jets. Instead, they contained, of all things, film. So much for that brilliant idea. And to compound problems, the Hurst shifter which had worked so beautifully at home wouldn't engage in second gear. Fortunately, though, it was a close ratio transmission, so we decided I could just rev it up a bit more in first and ignore second, shifting straight to third.

Fritz decided to solve my over carburetion problem by blocking off the center carburetor. He and Dick went to the local auto parts store for some gasket material, spark plugs, and some vacuum line to make my windshield wiper work. It looked like I was going to need it. Meanwhile, I borrowed some aluminum for a block off plate from the driver of one of the Porsches. By the time we finished with the carburetor and installing the plugs and vacuum line, it was raining lightly and most of the other racers had already headed to the hill climb at La Bufadora, which was approximately 14 miles south of Ensenada. As in years past, the purpose of the three-and-a-half-mile hill climb was to determine the starting order for Saturday's main event. As attendance wasn't mandatory, some of the open car drivers chose not to race in the rain and would start at the back of the pack.

We arrived with the Lincoln and the '49 just in time, with only a few cars still to go ahead of us. Fritz left ahead of Sally and me as we figured he would doubtless be faster. The rain had temporarily stopped, but the winding road was still somewhat slippery. We hadn't had time before leaving Ensenada to remove all of the tools, spare parts, etc, from the Lincoln's trunk, not to mention its extra 30 gallons of gas in the auxiliary tank, so Fritz took off with a few hundred extra pounds in his trunk.

After a one-minute interval, Sally and I took off. I drove somewhat conservatively on the wet road, not wanting to crash before the main event. We were happy just to be participating in the hill climb after missing it last year. When we reached the top of the hill we saw Fritz with a big grin on his face. He said, "It wasn't the fastest hill climb I've ever done, but it was definitely the most fun!" He described it as the rear wheels spinning wildly and the front wheels cocked back and forth like a champ car on a mile dirt track, and the rear end trying to swap ends with the front end all the way up the hill. All in all, it was an exhilarating ride. And all I wanted to do was to keep my car on the road - I guess I need more sprint car experience. The only problem he had was when he crested the last hill and overtook the Bug-Eyed Sprite that had started 60 seconds ahead of him. The Sprite was about to cross the finish line and was slowing rapidly when Fritz came flying over the hill. While the spectators looked on with a collective "Oh no!" - I imagine I've cleaned up the language a bit - Fritz calmly swerved off the road into the mud and gravel and slid sideways to a stop. He did a quick donut while looking over the sheer cliff right next to him that dropped to the ocean, and went to the parking area to wait for me. It was most definitely his idea of a good time.

After the hill climb was officially over, we were told to stay lined up on the way back to the hotel for a parade through Ensenada. Fritz and I traded cars for this event, as he wanted to check out my Ford, which was still fouling plugs, although not as badly as before. It wasn't long after the parade began that we realized the lead car in out group of seven or eight didn't have a clue where they were going. After several blocks of turns and U-turns, Fritz decided to take the '49 back to the hotel to work on it. Sally and I decided to follow the lost pack a little longer, laughing and enjoying the chase, before giving up and heading back to the hotel. Fun's fun, but I had a twenty-one month-old baby to attend to, as well as my other kids. I didn't want to impose on "Uncle Dick" for too long.

The drivers meeting was held that evening in the Hotel Corona lobby. The numbers for the race cars were given out, the car numbers correlating to the car's starting position, as determined by the hill climb. Fritz's number was 23, and I was assigned 32, right behind another Lincoln. Fritz, the other Lincoln, a Jag sedan and I were put into the vintage coupes over two liter class.

When we got up early the next morning, the first thing we did was to step out on the balcony to check the weather, which was beautiful. I had one small problem - a nasty case of the "touristas," "Montezuma's Revenge" or whatever you want to call it, it was inconvenient. To make matters worse, the toilet clogged up while Jason was using it, which traumatized him and further inconvenienced me. In all my adventures in Mexico I had never had to deal with that particular issue, but I certainly wasn't going to let it keep me from racing. I gulped down some Immodium and resolved not to eat or drink anything until after the race.

Fritz had problems of a different nature. It seemed every rubber O-ring in the Lincoln's Holley carburetor had completely disintegrated, causing major flooding problems. A quick search revealed that we had left the carb kit with all of the necessary replacement parts at home. The other cars were beginning to line up on Shoreline Boulevard in front of the hotel for the parade start of the race. Fritz worked feverishly disassembling and reassembling the carburetor trying to stop the leaks at the needles and seats and the transfer tube. He told me to go on out to the street to line up. While waiting for Fritz, Sally and I got the chance to check out some of the other race cars, which included a couple of Bug-Eyed Sprites, a few Allards, an assortment of Jags, some late model Porsches, a Lotus Super 7, our friend Charlie's Corvette, Ak Miller's car, the Shelby Mustang that had won the year before, and an assortment of late model cars for a total field of about 50.

Back in the parking lot, Fritz and Dick were trying everything they could think of - including wrapping pieces of string coated with "gorilla snot" (gasket cinch) around the needles and seats and transfer tube. He had the leaks stopped at the needles and seats, but was still working on the transfer tube when he was told the parking lot would close for the beginning of the race in one minute. He threw the carburetor back together and left the parking lot just in time. When he reached my car, he tried the gorilla snot and string on the transfer tube several more times. It just wasn't working, so he borrowed Dick's pocket knife and cut a couple of pieces from my windshield wiper vacuum line to make O-rings. The good news was the rain appeared to be over. The outer diameter was too large to fit in the float bowls, so Fritz, not having sandpaper, started grinding the rubber down on the sidewalk, which was coarser than the street. Dick, meanwhile, went back to the parking lot to get a file out of the Suburban. After a half-dozen attempts, Fritz was finally able to jam the transfer tube with its new O-rings into the float bowl. He finished reassembling the carburetor for what seemed like the tenth time and started the engine. Persistence and prayer paid off, and his flooding problem was at least temporarily solved. With three minutes to go before his scheduled starting time, Fritz jumped in the Lincoln, pulled on his helmet, and threaded his was through the remaining race cars to take his place two vehicles from the starting line.

Since the flooding carburetor had allowed who knows how much raw gas to get into the engine, the Lincoln had fouled about half of its spark plugs and was running less than impressively on the way through town to the official start at the 12 K marker on Highway 3. Once there, Fritz jumped out of the car, pulled the spark plugs and replaced them with the cleanest of the dirty plugs he had replaced earlier. These reject plugs got him running on about six cylinders. He didn't have enough time to try again, as he had to jump back into the car for the countdown and take off. About a mile down the road one of the dead cylinders cleaned out and the other one started firing intermittently, giving him seven-and-a-half cylinders, which beat the heck out of running on four or five.

Sally and I, meanwhile, were encouraged by the '49's performance. The plugs were staying clean and it wasn't overheating on the way up the hill to the starting line. We were ready to race.

There was a total of six speed stages, three on the way to Valle de la Trinidad, and three on the way back, meaning there was more flat out racing than not. The first speed section wound up through the mountains. Even at less than optimum performance, the Lincoln did its job well. Fritz had a great time sliding through the turns, tires squealing. While I drove a little more conservatively, Sally and I still had a lot of fun. We belted out *"Jeremiah was a bullfrog"* (Three Dog Night's "Joy to the World") at the top of our lungs, an old family tradition on road trips. I also got a kick out of passing a couple of the Bug-Eyed Sprites - they could out maneuver me in the turns, but didn't have my top end in the straightaways. Who needs second gear?

The checkpoints were well marked this year, with a flagman about 100 yards from the stopping point. The exception to this was the second checkpoint, which was a flying mile from a dead stop. After putting the pedal to the floor, it wasn't easy to stop in what seemed like about 50 yards. As we had been instructed not to go past a checkpoint, Fritz, with his usual flair, put the car sideways, did a donut in the mud and came back to the checkpoint. I don't think the Mexican officials knew quite what to make of him. I couldn't stop that fast either, but lacking Fritz's panache in such areas I did the best I could, jamming on the brakes and stopping about 50 feet past the official. He didn't seem to mind having to run to catch me - maybe after his experience with Fritz he was relieved by such a comparatively mild stop.

During the next transit stage, the '49 decided it was time to heat up. Visions of last year's problems flashed through my mind as I was forced to pull over to cool the engine. I jumped out, ran to the trunk, grabbed the water, opened the hood, poured a little water over the top of the top radiator tank to cool it down, waved to Ak Miller as he drove past, grabbed a rag, opened the radiator cap while standing as far away as possible to avoid being burned by the boiling water, dumped the rest of the water in, shut everything down, buckled in and took off. It seemed like this procedure took at least 15 minutes, but Sally assured me it only took two or three. The temperature was trying to climb again as we reached a water crossing, so I decided to let Mother Nature do the work for me. Instead of slowing to a crawl, we blasted through the six-inch deep crossing at about 35 or 40 mph, dropping the temperature from 200 degrees to 160 in a matter of seconds.

It wasn't much past that point when we saw our friend Charlie and his Corvette on the side of the road. He had blown a tire at about 170, which made for a very interesting ride. Unfortunately, he didn't have a spare. He later told me that as time went on he decided to lay on the ground by the car and have his navigator pretend to do CPR on him whenever any of the cars in his class would come by. As the concerned racer would slow down, Charlie would jump up and point at him, laughing.

The third speed section led us down out of the mountains to Valle de la Trinidad, the rest stop. When Fritz saw me, he grabbed me and gave me a big hug, exclaiming, "Baby, you made it!"

To which I replied, "Was there ever any doubt?"

We hadn't had time to gas the Lincoln before leaving Ensenada, but we had planned on getting some from Charlie's support crew. Unfortunately, they hadn't left

151

Ensenada before the road closed and were unable to get through. As Fritz was running critically low, I gave him all the money I had on me to buy some racing gas from the Jag sedan's crew, as the Jag had broken down and wouldn't need it. We added this to the Mexican gas he'd just bought at the local Pemex station and hoped it would be enough. As for the '49, not having a working gas gauge, we shook the car, heard gas sloshing in the tank and decided I had enough to get back. We also checked spark plugs, water, air, oil, etc., then headed back to the main road for the second half of the race.

Just when everything seemed to be going well, both of my big 12 volt batteries died and wouldn't even begin to crank the starter motor. The reason I had two batteries was that I ran a total loss electrical system -no generator to reduce drag on the engine - which had never given me a problem. Until then. Fritz hated to leave me, but had to, as his starting time was drawing near. Our friend Roger, also running a Lincoln, loaned me his jumper cables, but as he had a six volt car couldn't actually give me a jump. I started looking for possible candidates and asked a nearby local in a pickup truck for help in broken Spanish. Once he figured out what I was trying to ask, he was happy to help. Even though there were still several cars to go before my turn, I decided to move closer to the other racers, figuring I could get another jump if I had to shut it off. Not the best plan I ever had. Since I was having electrical problems, I couldn't run my electric fan, so, not surprisingly, the engine temperature started to climb and I had to turn it off. Thinking I could just get another jump, I went in search of another likely candidate, and found a gentleman from another support crew willing to help. The '49, however, refused to cooperate. No matter how long or how fast he revved his engine, or how much we wiggled the cable ends to insure good connection on the posts, it just wouldn't turn over. As I was pointed up hill and didn't think trying to bump start it in reverse would be very effective, in desperation we decided to pull start it. My hero from the other pit crew grabbed a tow rope from the back of the truck, and I prayed, "Please, Lord, I just want to finish the race." Just as the last car was leaving and the officials were ready to give up on me and leave, the truck gave a quick pull and my engine started purring like nothing had happened. The officials motioned me to hurry up, so with a quick thank you to both my rescuer and the Lord (prayer is a powerful thing) I hurried to the starting line and took off.

I knew the car had the potential to develop cooling problems especially since I couldn't run the electric fan, particularly at the check points where it would have to sit and idle. I also knew that I didn't dare shut off the engine, as most of the next 30 miles were all up hill, so bump starting wasn't a real option. A further source of concern was the weather. Dark clouds were gathering and rain was beginning to fall, and due to the Lincoln's custom-made carburetor O-rings, I didn't have working wipers. I could have pulled over and fiddled with the remaining vacuum line, but stopping didn't seem like a good option either. Occasionally I had to stick my head out the window as much as my five-point harness would allow in order to see where I was going. Never a dull moment, but at least we were still in the race, and gaining on the last cars which had left before us. As we overtook them, things started looking up. The rain mostly stopped, a cool breeze was blowing through the radiator keeping the engine temperature down, and the wait at the checkpoints, while a bit unnerving, weren't long enough to cause any real overheating problems. Aside from Sally having to hold the shifter in gear whenever I would back off while she was calling out the turns, things were going well.

153

Fritz, meanwhile, settled down to some serious racing. Catching up to the Lotus Super 7 they began playing leap frog, or rather, leap car, up the mountain road. There they were - the Lincoln, the heaviest car in the race at 4400 pounds, and the Lotus, the lightest car in the race at 1200 pounds, battling it out in the name of fun. All too soon for Fritz, he reached the 12 K marker and the official end of the race. From there, the cars were sent back into town in groups of ten or so to be put on display at the convention center.

Sometime later, Sally and I also reached the finish line. When we reached the convention center, most of the other racers were still there, bench racing and enjoying the complimentary *cervesas*. Fritz's face lit up when he saw the '49 pull in. Or maybe it was the free beer lighting him up. He pulled me close and said, "Honey, I'm so glad you made it!" I smiled warmly, touched by his concern until he added, "I really didn't feel like coming back to get you." When I asked him how the Lincoln had performed, he replied, "Well, the old gray mare ain't what she used to be, but she did good enough."

The awards dinner that evening was held at the convention center. Racing legend Carrol Shelby was there, signing autographs and trying to raise money for his favorite charity, the Children's Heart Fund. The food was amazing, from the grilled blue prawns to the Belgian chocolate brownies. The acoustics of the place, however, left much to be desired, making it difficult to hear everything that was being said. We made sure we could hear when it came time for the awards in our class, Vintage Coupes over two liters. Charlie, announcing the awards, began with third place, saying, "Now I know you guys think of racing as a macho sport, but there's this girl, just a petite little thing who drives a '49 Ford with a flathead in it." After presenting Sally and I with our trophy along with a certificate for a free Genuine Fischer harmonic balancer, it was time for second place. I was still trying to get over being called 'a petite little thing'. Second went to Roger, who had loaned me the jumper cables, and his Lincoln. When it came time to present first, Charlie said, "Now I like this guy. I always thought he was a better mechanic than driver. Fritz, will you come up here, please?" Charlie handed Fritz his trophy and an envelope, which he told him to open. Inside were ten $100 bills -the prize for first in class. This was a totally new experience, at least for me - winning money racing and not just spending it. The overall winner was Javier Espinoza in his Nissan 300ZX with an average speed of 102 mph. Javier had become something of a local hero in the past week, and his speed in the hill climb - a full thirty seconds faster than anyone else - had nearly made him a legend.

It was a happy group that returned to California the next day. Triumph in the face of adversity, coming home with two trophies,and actually winning money. What a great way to begin a racing season!

This was to be our last La Carrera Classic. The entry fees went up, the organizers changed the date to mid-summer, and we had shifted our focus a bit. We had always intended to return to road racing in Mexico, but never quite got there. But, with Fritz, there was always something new in store.

Chapter 13

It's Not Easy Keeping Dirt Clean

Fritz and I were very excited when we learned that SCTA had arranged with the military to allow us to run on historic Muroc Dry Lake, which is on Edwards Air Force Base in the Mojave Desert. As this is where a lot of top secret testing is held and where the space shuttle landed, this took some definite negotiations and promises on the SCTA's part. The rules were made very clear to the racers multiple times: Don't spill anything on the lake bed surface, no tent stakes, including those to hold EZ Ups and other canopies, don't wander away from the designated area, and don't look at anything or photograph anything that is not within the designated area. And as always, be considerate of the desert tortoises.

The track itself was 1.5 miles in length, to make it different from El Mirage's 1.3 mile track. Two tenths of a mile may not seem like much, but it actually does allow for a greater speed to be achieved.

Our friend Keenan made the first run down the track on his 1942 military 45 c.i. Harley, which seemed very appropriate. Keenan did not endear himself to the racers waiting to run next when he left the starting line hard, leaving a cloud of dust to settle over everyone behind him. I know of one former crew chief who wanted to pound him into the ground like the forbidden tent stakes, but decided against it. Actually, I think he was more talked out of it. Or perhaps he was physically restrained until he calmed down. As per usual, I split crew duties between Keenan, Fritz and our friend Terry with his BSA. Fritz and Terry both made their runs, as well as the other competitors. The race meet was progressing well, until the wind came up.

While I loved Muroc and would go back in a heartbeat if it were still available, it had two setbacks that made it challenging. First was the wind. Wind is not uncommon in the California desert, but strong wind shuts down a race meet due to safety concerns. The other problem is the dirt is exceptionally fine and powdery. El Mirage is a dirty place to have fun, but with Muroc the dirt gets into every pore and crevice of everyone and everything on the lake bed, especially with a 40 mile per hour wind to drive it. SCTA decided that to commemorate the racers return to Muroc, they would invite a number of street rods for a car show. Once the wind picked up, the beautiful shiny street rods all turned the same color - dirt brown. The dust storm was so bad, everyone had to find cover, and you literally couldn't see more than a few feet in front of you.

This same wind persisted into the night. I don't know if you've ever tried to set up a tent with no stakes allowed in a 30-mph wind, but I have, and let me assure you it is not easy, especially in the pitch black of a moonless desert night. Fritz decided to move the truck to a more strategic location to better block the wind. The only problem with this was we had an issue with the pressure regulator on the '71 Ford's oil pump and the excessive pressure caused our oil filter to blow off the engine, spewing motor oil all over the ground. Keep in mind the air force had made it clear that they would be unhappy with so much as a cigarette butt left on the ground after the races. So, there we were in the dark and the howling wind, trying to clean who knew how much oil off the dirt while simultaniously trying to keep the tent from blowing away. And this is what we did for fun?

When we left the next afternoon, wondering what had ever possessed us to race in such an inhospitable place, we knew that if they held another meet at Muroc we would be there. In fact, over the course of the next five or so years of competing at Muroc, we wondered what possessed us to race there every year, but there was never any question about whether we would go back. When security and other issues finally shut it down, we missed it. Even though it has been two decades since I drove the '49 Ford out there - we took it in '98 - there is still Muroc silt in some of the crevasses in my car.

For some obscure reason that I neither recall nor understand, we had some extra money during Speed Week in 1995. Fritz decided it would be a good idea to use that money to change classes with the bike, and set as many records as we could afford. While some of them weren't particularly sensational, we did set four records nonetheless, making the impound area practically our second pit. Yes, we had a different idea about what a 'home away from home' was. After years of beating our heads against the proverbial wall, this year things seemed to go remarkably smoothly. After setting either our third or fourth record that week, I jokingly said, "Well, another day, another record."

Fritz responded, "Gayle, don't jinx us!"

We could only afford three class changes and still be able to make it home, so towards the end of the meet we tried to bump the records we had set earlier in the week. That was also the year Fritz had set up a shower head attached to the wooden stake sides he had added to the truck, using an electric fuel pump to pump water out of a can in the truck's bed. He was hot and sweaty after one particular run, so he stripped out of his leathers, along with everything else, on the edge of the return road and proceeded to take a shower, while I just shook my head. At least it was mostly deserted down there. Fritz always said he was shy, but I never really saw that side of him.

The shower worked better at Bonneville than at El Mirage. The salt absorbed the water, in general, but the El Mirage dirt turned to slimy, slippery mud. A month later when Fritz tried to give three-year-old Chris a shower at El Mirage - at least Fritz was in shorts that time - they both slipped and fell and became entirely covered with mud. It was not exactly the result he had in mind, but it was hilarious to watch.

They say mud baths are good for the complexion...

Chapter 14

Starter? Starter? We Don't Need No Stinking Starter

During the winter our friend Jim L. wanted to know if Fritz would ride one of his motorcycles, a Harley WR tank shifter, at the AHRMA vintage road races during Bike Week in Daytona, Florida. Fritz, who had always wanted to run at Daytona International Speedway, jumped at the chance. We helped Jim build the bike, Fritz joined AHRMA, and we got ready to make the 2300-mile trip to Daytona Beach. One of the requirements before you could run at Daytona was to run in another AHRMA sanctioned race first. The only one available and practical was at Roebling Road near Savannah, Georgia about a week before. Our 14-year-old sons, Andy and Zeke, were unable to go due to school conflicts, so we made arrangements for Andy to stay with a friend. I got Jason's homework in advance from his school - it's easier when you're dealing with a second grader. We decided to take our '69 Volkswagen bus and a 55-gallon drum of Pick-A-Part gas, which we figured would at least get us part of the way there. The day before we had to leave the starter went out in the VW. Fritz said, "Don't worry, it's easy to bump start. Besides, it's freeway all the way there. We'll fix it when we get to Georgia."

We caravanned with Jim and his girl-friend at the

time, Lori, and her six-year-old daughter Ashley, who were riding in Jim's truck with the motorcycles in the back. Jim was also taking a motorcycle of his that had been owned and raced by racing legend Floyd Emde, which he was going to ride during an exhibition at the speedway. So, off we went, me pushing the bus to start it while Fritz popped the clutch, then Fritz stopping so I could get in. The Pick-A-Part gas got us well into Texas. As it was a good clean drum and we had no further need of it, we left it a rest stop with a 'free' sign on it, hoping someone could use it. To be specific, it was the Stink Creek rest stop near Noodle Dome Road, as I recall. A name like that kind of sticks in your memory, but I'm not guaranteeing time hasn't modified my recollection.

We finally reached the track in Georgia, although somewhere around that time the clutch in the VW bus went out. Fritz decided he didn't have time to fix it right then, but assured me we would take care of it when we got to Deland, Florida, which was where race headquarters was located. This meant that when we bump started it he had to have it in first gear and I had to jump in while it was moving. It also meant he would shift by the sound of the engine without benefit of a clutch. Coming to a red light at the top of a hill was also problematic, so Fritz had to anticipate this and go in circles in whatever nearby parking lot he could find so that we didn't actually have to stop moving. Naturally, we had to be careful that we always parked facing down hill. When we got to Roebling Road, Jim towed us in with a rope, because the stop and go traffic at the entrance made a normal entrance impossible for us.

Roebling Road itself was a beautiful track, surrounded by pines and greenery. Fritz was very eager to ride, and enjoyed the race immensely, getting the opportunity to size up the competition. He had a minor tantrum

161

before the race when something wasn't going according
to his plan, but we worked it out. His fellow competitors
were for the most part extremely nice people who gave a
very favorable impression. I don't remember what position he finished, but once the race was over, it was time to
head to Deland.

We didn't have enough money to stay in the Holiday
Inn itself, which was race headquarters, so we stayed in
our VW in the parking lot, a theme which we would repeat. Actually, we started a trend - in the two subsequent
years we ran Daytona, we saw more and more people do
the same. Jim and Lori did have a room, however, so in
the morning we went up to see if they were ready to head
out to the track. Little Ashley asked eight-year-old Jason
if he liked her shirt. Being a boy, he said something to the
effect of, "I dunno."

Ashley turned to her mother and said, "Mom! Jason
doesn't like it! I have to change!" After quickly convincing
Jason to tell her he liked the shirt for the sake of expediency, we were able to get on with our day. The seven of
us crammed into Jim's truck and went to the speedway,
looking for tech inspection. The guy we talked to at the
gate didn't know what we were talking about, but sent us
into the infield across the track. I have to admit, coming
onto the track at Daytona International Speedway was
one of the most awe-inspiring experiences Fritz and I ever
had. I've been a NASCAR fan since I watched Cale Yar-
borough and Bobby Allison duke it out at the finish line of
the 1979 Daytona 500, and being on that track, looking at
the 37-degree banking, feeling the history, was something
I'll never forget.

Tech inspection turned out to be somewhere else
entirely, which we eventually figured out and got through.
The race itself, a few days later, was fun to watch, and the
fulfillment of a dream for Fritz. Having to be in the 'hot

pit' to get him ready was pretty cool for me as well - it felt very special. Granted he didn't win, as most of his fellow competitors had way more experience there than he did, but just being there participating was incredible enough. From the pits, we also got to see some of the vintage greats run, like Don Vesco and Dick Mann, among others.

We went to a couple of motorcycle swap meets which were held during Bike Week, and at one there was a large fenced off pond complete with alligator. Fritz told little Ashley to stay away from the pond because the alligator ate dogs and little kids. Lori's daughter not only took this to heart, but did her absolute best to inform every member of the public about the dangerous gator. And I mean *everyone*. I was the one appointed to stay with the kids while Fritz, Jim and Lori were browsing through the swap meet, so I can speak with authority. She would jump out in front of unsuspecting swap meet attendees and greet them with, "There's an alligator in the pond that eats dogs and little kids!" They would either smile because she was cute or try to keep a straight face and say okay, or look at me with a bemused expression on their faces. No matter what the response, she was undaunted in her self-appointed public service announcement. And to her credit, during the two or three hours we were there, not one person or dog climbed the eight-foot chain link fence surrounding the pond to swim with the gator.

Back at the Holiday Inn parking lot, since driving without a clutch or starter was challenging, we did a lot of walking. We were very fortunate there was a Publix market across the street and a Walmart down a couple of blocks. We even found an auto parts store a block or so past Walmart. Unfortunately, Fritz didn't like the clutch they had and it was going to take them too long to get a starter. So, it looked like we were going to push start the bus all the way back to California at the end of the week.

Diary of a Racer's Wife

One night we decided we wanted ice cream sundaes. Since we had no way of keeping ice cream frozen in a Volkswagen in Florida, we chose to forego dinner and just eat sundaes. Trying to justify feeding my children ice cream for dinner while shopping, we added chopped peanuts, which are a source of protein, and maraschino cherries, which are fruit, at least sort of. Of course, we also had chocolate syrup and whipped cream because it just wouldn't be an ice cream sundae otherwise. Even though I wouldn't advocate this as a steady diet, between the four of us I can guarantee none of the half gallon of vanilla ice cream went to waste.

All too soon it was time to start pushing the VW back toward Southern California. A storm came through the panhandle of Florida, creating a sheet of water on the flat highways. Hydroplaning down the highway was not the most fun thing ever, but Fritz's skill and my prayers got us through. It also got very cold in the VW bus, so we stopped at a rest stop to warm ourselves up under the hand dryers. The heater, being in the back, didn't really work well enough to heat the bus, but Jason left one of his flip flops in front of the vent, and it was sufficiently hot to reduce the synthetic rubber sandal to about half of its original size.

The next day we stopped at a private museum owned by an acquaintance of Jim's in Texas. He had an absolutley amazing vehicle collection. And then came San Antonio. Don't get me wrong, I like San Antonio, I just can't go there without getting lost. Interstate 10, which stretches all the way from the coast of California at Santa Monica to the coast of Florida at St. Petersburg, takes a sharp right in the middle of San Antonio, and if you can't get in the right lane quickly enough, you miss it. I know this, because we did, and on more than one occasion. It was at this point that we lost Jim and Lori as well - they made the turn on the 10. I still didn't have a cell phone at that time, so they kept going, figuring we were grown-ups and could find our way home. While we were lost in San Antonio, we did find the Alamo, and toured it, which was very interesting, as Fritz and I both loved history. And, yes, now I can say, "I remember the Alamo."

After finally finding the correct freeway again, we continued toward home. Living in the VW bus for two weeks must have taken its toll on our appearance. We stopped for gas at a station in Midland, Texas, where at that time, you paid after you pumped. We went in to pay for our gas only to find some unknown Texan Samaritan had seen us and paid for our gas when he went in to pay for his. We were very surprised, and, in all honesty, grateful, as our money was starting to run a bit thin, and even more so when the proprietor of the gas station told us to get a drink for ourselves and our kids out of the refrigerator on him, which was very kind. We told him we could pay, but he insisted, so we thanked him and once more push started the bus, heading for home.

The only other incident of note occurred on Interstate 8 in California when we broke the generator belt a few miles outside of Ocotillo. Without this belt, the bus wouldn't go. Fritz tried using a piece of rope as a makeshift belt, but that was unsuccessful. About this time a highway patrolman pulled up and told us we couldn't stay parked on the edge of the freeway. Fritz explained the situation to him, and he generously offered to give Fritz a ride to the auto parts store in Ocotillo, but told him he'd have to find his own way back. This worked out quite nicely as Fritz was able to get the belt, get a ride back on a frontage road, install it, and we were finally on our way again, reaching home with a grand total of $8.00 to our names, give or take 50 cents.

You know the expression one door closes and another opens? I couldn't help but think of that. As I mentioned earlier, we had reluctantly decided to stop attending the La Carrera Classic, but now we had Daytona, at least for the next few years. El Mirage and Bonneville were of course a normal part of life, as now was Muroc. I sometimes still miss racing in Mexico, though, - it has a unique flavor all its own.

Later that year Jim asked Fritz if he would like to run his Harley tank shifter again, this time at the Ed Kretz TT in Del Mar. The initials 'TT' stand for 'Tourist Trophy', which I'm sure made sense when the name was conceived. Fritz hadn't run a TT in a long time, but was eager to do so, even though the brakes on the WR weren't exactly working. I'd never actually seen a TT event before and at this particular track, I viewed it as the predecessor to modern day motocross. He had a blast, and won his class. That sounds fairly impressive, but I think he may have been in a class by himself, in more ways than one. It was while we were watching the AMA main event later that day that I met AMA legend Sammy "the Flying Flea" Tanner. I'm afraid I acted like a 15-year-old girl meeting a rock star. "Oh, Mr. Tanner, you were always my favorite!" I gushed. This was true, although in my shallowness it wasn't all appreciation for his riding skill, which was considerable - he was a good-looking man.

Chapter 15

Reaching the Point Was Not a Pinnacle

Fritz had such a great time road racing at Daytona that he decided we needed to run one of our own bikes there, so, he scrounged enough spare parts to put together a Harley KR road racer. I make this sound easier than it was. When a project caught hold of Fritz, it became his single focus, to the exclusion of things like earning enough money to pay the bills, etc. He also thought we could deliver a 1954 Lincoln to a friend in Georgia on the way, and kill two birds with one stone. We decided son Andy needed to go with us that year, even though the high school was not in favor of him being gone for two weeks. However, there is more to education than just what you can get from text books, and Andy was an extremely bright kid. Fritz built a motorcycle carrier to sit on the front of the car trailer. We loaded the Harley, which he nicknamed "Old Black Magic," Dick A.'s '54 Lincoln and as much Pick-A-Part gas as we could and hooked it up to our '72 Ford one-ton crew cab pickup with a camper, nicknamed the "Green Monster." After the experience with the VW, I was hoping not to have to push that one.

We hadn't made it far - the mountains near Alpine, still in San Diego County, to be exact - when Fritz noticed the truck's C-6 transmission temperature climbing. It

concerned him to the point that he made the decision to
turn around and leave the Lincoln at home, figuring we
would just have to call Dick and let him know we weren't
going to be able to deliver his car that year. Even though,
as another racing friend put it, "time was our enemy,"
we figured not having to go to Georgia would compensate for the time we lost turning around and unloading
the car. In case I haven't made it clear already, getting
somewhere early was never really in Fritz's program. He
always worked to the last possible second trying to build,
repair and improve the things we needed for our racing
ventures. So, after unloading the Lincoln, making a phone
call, and repositioning our load, we were off again.

 This year, thanks to a small inheritance from Fritz's
aunt, we had a little more money than normal to work
with, so Fritz was eager to check out the swap meets that
were a part of bike week. For us, driving to Florida was
a three-day trip - one day to get to Texas, one day to get
through Texas, and one day to get from Texas to Florida.
Just outside Pensacola we blew the left front tire on the
Green Monster. Since we only had one spare for the truck,
we had to buy a tire in Pensacola. This may not sound
particularly odd to most people, but as I've said, Fritz believed in putting used tires on everything and using them
up. This was the first new tire he had purchased since
1985, when he bought a pair for the Chevy Luv truck
he had given me. I'm still not sure if he bought them to
impress me early in our relationship or if he couldn't find
any used tires the correct size.

 Soon enough we were back on our way and made our
way to the Holiday Inn parking lot in Deland. We actually
knew where tech inspection was this year, so we made our
way there and managed to get through that. Daytona being one of AHRMA's premier events, they got pretty picky.
Appearances of both the bikes and the riders were very

important to the inspectors, and stainless-steel safety wire was expected to glisten even on bolts that didn't ordinarily loosen. Speaking of appearances, one of Fritz's big complaints was he hadn't taken the time to cut his hair before we left home. Fritz had naturally wavy hair, and left untended it would encompass his head like a fuzzy mushroom. On one particular day it was bushing out on both sides of his face and innocent little Chris looked up at him and exclaimed, "Daddy, you look just like Krusty the Clown!"

Chris's observation was not well received by his dad, and for the rest of the trip Fritz continued to grouse about his hair, saying, "I can't believe you didn't make me cut my hair before we left!" For those of us not having a bad hair day, though, it was hilarious, and became a bit of a running joke with me and the kids. Sometimes thinking about it I couldn't keep a straight face, even when it was more prudent to do so.

The race itself was a lot of fun. Fritz loved running on the high banks, but you had to be going fast enough to stay up there or gravity would win and drag you to the bottom of the track. He ended up finishing 11th that year, and was proud of it.

Fritz had a good time at the swap meets. His big purchase was a Druin supercharger for our '75 850 Norton Commando. My big purchase was a ten-pound bag of pecans with the shells pre-cracked - they gave us something to munch on that lasted through a couple of states on the way home. The kids and I went to Disney World while Fritz went to another swap meet, with the plan being to meet him outside the princess castle. This didn't work out so well, as I later learned he was on one side and I on another, so I kept sending the kids on rides while I waited... and waited. We finally met up outside the park at the end of the day, although earlier I started to entertain the idea

of camping out with the kids at Mister Toad's Wild Ride,
if I couldn't find him.

We decided to stop by the Pensacola Air Museum on
the way home. Good decision - it was very well done and
extremely interesting. Once out of Florida, we started
having problems with the Green Monster. The oil con-
sumption, which hadn't been lovely before, grew to the
need of a quart or so every 100 miles, then eventually
every 50 miles. But we had more problems besides needing to buy stock in Texaco. The water pump began acting
up. As we had a 1968 engine in the truck, and it was a
one-year only engine design, it was problematic. We started scouring junkyards, but with no success. There just
weren't many '68 Fords with 460's around. In Mississippi
we had even more problems, and by the time we hit Baton
Rouge we had to stop at an auto parts store, get what we
needed and fix the truck in the parking lot.

While Fritz and I were working on the truck I sent
the kids into the Burger King next door to eat. When they
came back a short time later, Andy told me, "I'm never
taking them in anywhere again!"

Apparently, his littlest brother had belched so loudly that it stopped all conversation in the restaurant, drawing all eyes to them, and causing the lady working in the
dining area to say, "Well, my goodness, honey!"

Fritz and I finally got the truck patched up enough
to limp back home. And sure enough, when we got to San
Antonio we got lost again. Fritz was pretty grumpy by
this time, but we all survived it, and eventually found
the freeway. We continued toward home, although having to stop every 50 miles to add oil was not conducive to
making good time. Ultimately it did not bode well for the
longevity of the engine, which later threw a connecting
rod on the way to a San Diego Roadster Club meeting.

That's a story in itself. It was the first time I ever

heard an engine throw a rod. It was like there was suddenly an angry little man with a big hammer inside, growing louder and louder, followed by dead silence as we coasted to the side of the freeway. It was also the first time I ever had to scale a six-foot chain link fence so I could hike under the freeway to get to a pay phone on the other side. It sounds like the beginning of a bad joke. "Why did the SDRC President cross the road?" But back to the long trip home from Daytona. Perhaps 'long' isn't the correct word. 'Arduous' or 'painfully slow and frustrating' are far more accurate. I'd like to say I saw a lot more scenery having to stop so frequently, but somehow that isn't where I was focused. It was indescribably good to finally reach home, and we had a whole year to forget what a pain in the neck the truck had been and only remember the good parts.

Later that spring we decided to run the AHRMA races at Laguna Seca. We picked up Zeke from his Mom's in Santa Cruz and headed to the track. What an amazing place! Zeke brought his off-road skateboard, which was fun for him on the hills. I once more helped Fritz in the hot pits for his ride, making Andy and Zeke watch nine-year-old Jason and four-year-old Chris. Fritz loved the track, especially the corkscrew. During some of the races, the boys and I sat on a grassy hill near there, as that was where some of the best racing was happening. At other times, we were hanging out with Don Vesco and one of his good friends. Not only was Don a gifted racer, he was really funny. I was helping remove some stickers from his buddy's bike, and it wasn't going entirely well. Just to tease me Don said, "Look at what you've done to his bike!" It was a magical time at the races there that year. It wasn't the hallowed ground of Daytona, but for pure fun it remains one of my favorite tracks.

After a number of years of sleeping in tents at Bonneville, having a used camper on the back of our '71 Ford pickup was the height of luxury for me. I still had to cook and clean, just like at home, but at least there was a place for the kids to be in the shade during the day. Fritz was never one to quit using something until it was completely used up, and this camper was no exception. Unfortunately for the longevity of the camper, it had to be removed from the truck on a regular basis so the truck could be used as, well, a truck. Between that and the rough roads on which we travelled, our driveway being perhaps the roughest, it began to literally fall apart at the seams. This became obvious during Speed Week when we went to the grocery store late one evening. We were parked on a slant, and Jason's yo-yo rolled out through a gap in the wall and down across the parking lot. Since Jason loved his yo-yo, we had to chase it down the hill through the cars in the dark. Obviously, we had to be cautious for the remainder of the trip not to lose anything else, like tools, food, kids, and so on. As a side note, the next time the camper was unloaded from the truck, it was done at the landfill.

We had taken the road racer with us to Bonneville, so we could run an AHRMA race at Sears Point immediately following Speed Week. This sounded like a good idea before we left, but the reality wasn't as ideal. Fritz and I were facing some serious challenges in our relationship, and both of us were feeling the strain. Combine that with everything we had gone through to get to Bonneville, and the drain of the week itself, the result was we were just flat too wiped out to enjoy the racing. We put the Sportster in the bike show they had there in the Competition Class. Since it had just set a record and still had salt falling off of it, and it was a pretty cool piece, we won. Speaking of salt falling off of things, we hadn't taken the time to 'desalt' the truck, as Fritz was in a hurry to make it to the track on time, and the moist air at Sears Point

172

was causing huge chunks to fall off onto the parking lot. It looked like we had been caught in a blizzard. We were very politely asked to clean up the mess we were creating, as they didn't want the salt to contaminate the estuary. Completely appreciating their position, we did so, although this presented its own set of challenges trying to dispose of it properly. I used a paper plate folded in half as a makeshift dust pan, and carried load after load of salt to the nearest trash can. Eventually we had our salty mess sufficiently under control, and got back to the business of racing. We were tired, we were grumpy, and neither of us could get excited about the race. Fritz ran the event, didn't finish well, but did finish. All in all, it was real, it was fun, but it just wasn't real fun.

We continued to run El Mirage that fall, and during the course of the year sorted out our marital issues. It took several years for our relationship to fully recover, but we were a team, both at the races and at home, and we stuck together no matter what.

Chapter 16

Not Talladega Nights, but Daytona Daze

Our 1998 Daytona adventure started early that year. Remember when I mentioned the creek that runs across our driveway? Most of the time, this is not a problem. Sometimes, as I've said, it's another story. This is one of those stories.

The winter of 1997-1998 was shaping up to be another wet one, where the creek reached flood stage on more than one occasion. Needless to say, it's not particularly crossable even by truck when it is like that. We knew another storm was coming which would prevent us from getting the truck and trailer across to go to Daytona. We were taking a different truck this year, our '71 Ford three-quarter ton pickup with a camper. We were again going to attempt to take Dick A.'s Lincoln to him in Georgia on our way, so once more we had the Lincoln loaded on the car trailer, along with the Harley and enough Pick-A-Part gas to get us there. We made arrangements with a good friend to leave everything at her place for a couple of days in case the river came up. This turned out to be a good call, because it rose to the point we couldn't cross it without a submarine. Not having a sub handy on the day we needed to leave, we hiked about a mile through the brush following the power company line road to where we knew one of the neighbors had a little metal car, for lack of a better term, on a cable that we could climb into and pull ourselves across the creek to the other side. Other than catching my jeans on a rusty bolt and tearing them, this went fairly smoothly, and we were able to hike back down the road to the end of our driveway, where we had moved the truck just before it started raining. So, it only took walking two miles to get 200 feet to the other side of the creek, but we've done more for less good reason.

This particular Ford had a manual transmission, so there was no real concern climbing the local mountains with a load. It turned out to be a real plus when we got to Georgia. Dick's version of "just a little ways out of town" turned out to be 20 or so miles up a steep, narrow, winding mountain road. Beautiful, yes, but not exactly what we had anticipated. Eventually, just as darkness was falling, we found his place and delivered the car. On our way back down the mountain Fritz remembered that he had left 10 or 15 gallons of Pick-A-Part gas in the trunk of the Lincoln, and was seriously considering finding somewhere to turn truck and trailer around. This would have been no mean feat to go back up the mountain in the pitch black night to get it, but for once I was able to dissuade him, even though it meant buying more gas.

The race at Daytona was a little more stressful this year. Our camping spot in the Deland Holiday Inn parking lot was still fine, although there were even more parking lot campers than previous years. Tech inspection didn't go particularly well, as the inspectors weren't pleased with the condition of Fritz's leathers, but we finally made it through. Our big problem right after that ordeal was that we couldn't figure out why the bike wasn't running right. We checked all the normal probabilities without success. We were working on it in the parking lot until three a.m. the morning of the race - me holding the drop light while Fritz tried everything he could think of to fix it. I learned that it is humanly possible to sleep while standing, because I literally fell asleep holding that drop light and stayed on my feet. I knew I was asleep because he would yell at me because I wasn't holding the light where he wanted it, and his yelling kept waking me up. We finally had to give up and go to bed for two hours before we had to go to the track.

The other problem was the KR engine was still blown up from a racing related incident at El Mirage that I prefer not to go into, mostly because it made me extremely angry and I don't want to be unkind to those involved. Because of this, Fritz had put the KH engine into the road race chassis. They look nearly identical unless you really know what you are looking at, the KH being slightly taller through the cylinder to accommodate the longer stroke. The longer stroke meant more displacement, and the larger displacement meant we were running an engine larger than our class allowed. There was no option for a bigger class at that time, so the bottom line was if he wanted to run we would be cheating. Fritz didn't figure he would win anyway, but, if by some chance he had, he would have confessed and not accepted first place. I know this because we discussed it prior to leaving for Daytona when I found out what he was going to do.

Well, this never became an issue, because someone actually did know what they were looking at and told the officials, who came over to inspect the bike. Fritz knew why they were there, looked them straight in the eyes and told them the truth - that he didn't have time to rebuild the KR and really wanted to run, so he put the bigger motor in. No whining, no excuses - I've got to say I didn't always agree with him, but when it came to things like this, the man had class. The officials understood his position, but couldn't let him participate in the race. They did let him run practice, so Fritz at least got some track time.

The bike still wasn't running worth beans, but he got it running well enough to keep it up on the banking. It took us until Bonneville that summer to figure out what was wrong after checking everything I don't even know how many times, he found a wasp lodged in a passage in the S&S Super B carburetor. Yes, a bee in the Super B.

After the vintage racing was over, we decided to go to Cape Kennedy for a day on our way home, as that was something I had always wanted to do. When I was little I wanted to be an astronaut. Actually, I still do.

Next, we decided to go explore the other coast of Florida. We made our way onto Santa Maria Island, and even though there were signs posted saying no overnight camping, Fritz found a little vacant lot where a somewhat recent hurricane had demolished a house and decided we would stay there for the night. Shortly after midnight, we were awakened by one of the local police, who very politely told us we couldn't camp there overnight. He then suggested we might be able to stay in the parking lot of the local Holiday Inn. Fritz and I gave each other a sideways glance and politely thanked him. As we were getting in the cab of the truck to leave, we burst out laughing, because we were being told to go stay in the Holiday Inn parking lot. Fritz looked over at me and said, "Do you think he knows who we are?"

While we were still at Daytona, Don Vesco had noticed our now empty car trailer and asked it we would mind picking up about six motorcycles for him in northern Florida and hauling them back to California. He lived about 40 miles from us, so delivery to him wasn't an issue. We told him it was no problem, and went in search of the bikes in question. I can't remember the name of the town, but if I ever get rich I'm figuring it out and moving there - everybody had a private airplane hanger next to their garage, and you could taxi down the street to the runway to take off. Coolest place ever! The gentleman that Don had purchased the motorcycles from was very informative and gracious, and soon we had them loaded and were on our way. We had to stop in Pensacola at the air museum again. Fritz was convinced he hadn't seen it all the first time, and it is an interesting place.

Other than getting lost as usual in San Antonio, the rest of the journey was without particular incident. We always intended to go back to Daytona, the next time with a legal bike, but got sidetracked by other things and never made it back.

Several months later, Fritz decided he wanted to run the road racer at the Harley flat track event at Costa Mesa. I was planning on going with him, but Chris had the chicken pox and I had to stay with him. Not to worry, though, by this time Andy and Jason were well trained as pit crew. Even though Fritz hadn't run a flat track event in 20 years or so, he made it into the semi-finals with no problem. In the semis, though, another competitor, riding an XR750, got a bit aggressive and center-punched Fritz's bike, sending Fritz flying. There is no pain while you are racing, however, and Fritz was able to transfer into the main event, where he won. The announcer made a comment with something to the effect of Fritz risking a $40,000 motorcycle for a two-dollar trophy, but he was pretty proud of that trophy. After the adrenaline rush was over, he realized the incident in the semi-finals had injured his wrist and had cracked a couple of ribs. He still took Jason and Andy to Six Flags Magic Mountain the next day, as we had free tickets and he wanted to take advantage of them and treat the kids, in spite of his pain.

Bonneville was such a normal part of our lives that a lot of them tend to blend together. Spend the majority of the summer working on the Harley, spend a couple of days repairing whatever truck we were going to drive, spend way more time loading than it reasonably should have taken, drive through the night until Fritz couldn't see straight, and then either I, or eventually Jason, would take over. We'd get to the salt a day later than we wanted, and spend the next week dedicated to the pursuit of speed, usually camping at Road's Bend in the evenings, because it was closer when we had to be there early for return record runs, which, of course, was the whole point.

That being said, Speed Week of 1998 stands out to me. We were in the process of freshening up our 1000 cc Sportster engine to run in the K Model chassis, which we had been doing at both El Mirage and Muroc that season. Fritz was going to modify the heads a bit and change the cams. I was glancing through the rule book again, and happened to notice something I had missed earlier in the season - the .020 overbore which had previously been allowed wasn't in the book anymore. As our cylinders were already bored to .010 over, this wasn't going to work. After a few frantic calls to the head of the tech committee, who drily commented, "The rule book came out last spring," and being unable to find any decent standard bore cylinders, at least any that were cost effective, we decided to go with what was available to us and 'fluff up' the 900 cc Sportster engine that we had built for El Mirage when the 900 class still existed. That particular engine had been sitting on the porch covered up for a while, ever since SCTA increased the class displacement to 1000 cc. It was small for the class, obviously, but it was there, and as usual, time was our enemy.

For most of the next week, our friend Keenan's machine shop became Fritz's home away from home. Fritz usually didn't get home from there until sometime in the middle of the night or early morning. Rebuilding another engine wasn't our only problem. Our '71 Ford pickup, our transportation to and from the salt, decided

179

to develop a howl coming from the area of the rear end. Fritz felt around and found the parts hot to the touch, which seemed to confirm his suspicions that the rear end was going to fail. Not to panic, though, we had another three-quarter ton truck of similar vintage stored at a friend's place, so the logical thing for us to do was go there and remove the center section from that rear end. We stopped on the way there for a five-minute visit with a friend, which turned into an hour and a half. By the time we actually got to where our truck was stored, we were lying in the weeds under the truck in the dark, groping around to pull the center section out. We were able to manage this before our flashlight went dead, and I only thought a few times about how rattlesnakes, which are common in the area, come out after dark to hunt. At least there was a full moon and we accomplished our mission, getting home just before midnight.

The next day, five days before we had planned to leave, we pulled the inspection cover and decided the differential needed shims for proper gear spacing. Andy, now 17, couldn't locate any in town, so we decided to pull them from the rear end we had removed from our truck. When we pulled the inspection cover off, we realized, much to our chagrin, that there was absolutely nothing wrong with that differential. We finally worked out that the howl was from a U-joint we had replaced only a few months earlier. The dump tubes on the mufflers had rusted off, and the hot exhaust was blasting directly onto it. We reinstalled our perfectly good rear end and corrected the faulty U-joint, adjusted the exhaust a bit, and resumed work on the bike.

When we pulled the engine from its resting place on the porch and lifted it onto the workbench, we noticed some water dribbling out of the gear case cover. Even though it had been covered, apparently the porch roof had leaked and the cover had leaked and water had funneled directly into the hole where the magneto had been removed. Upon inspection, we learned some good news and some bad news. The Andrews X cams were still in good shape. Now for the bad news. The flywheels, crankpin, rod bearings, etc., were a rusty mess. So, with four days to go, the engine had to come completely apart and be rebuilt. Meanwhile, Keenan's bike was also still apart, although Terry's BSA was just about back together. The next few days kind of blurred together, as Fritz would haul himself home from Keenan's shop around dawn and catch a few hours of sleep before heading back to San Diego to start all over.

Finally, or perhaps I should say all too soon, it was Thursday, our scheduled day of departure. Terry had taken a quick drive up to Glendora to pick up a part for Keenan's electronic ignition. Fritz had our Harley home and mostly together, with the exception of the oil tank and a few miscellaneous hoses and oil lines. Our little group met at our house just before dark. We finished some welding on our trailer and loaded as much as we could remember, which wasn't much, at that point. Around midnight, we headed for the salt - Fritz and I, with Jason and Chris in the Ford, Terry in his Dodge pickup with Keenan's nephew Will, Keenan in his Datsun pickup. Andy and his friend Ash would be joining us up there a bit later in the week. We made it as far as the Walmart parking lot in Rancho Cucamonga, about 60 miles from our house, before we had to sleep for a couple of hours.

Other than occasionally seeing highway lanes that didn't exist because we were so tired, it was a fairly uneventful trip. It was Terry and Will's first pilgrimage to the salt, so we paused as we came over the pass to let them see the vast white expanse in the valley below. For me, it felt like being home again.

Diary of a Racer's Wife

Saturday, we set up our pit, attended the mandatory drivers meeting, got Terry and Keenan through inspection, and finished assembling our bike. The weather was perfect and the salt was as good as I had seen it in the 14 years I had been going there. It was also really nice to get more than a few hours of sleep that night - I think we managed 6 or 7. Sunday was another beautiful day. Terry qualified for a record on his BSA at 113. The existing record in his class was 109. Keenan thought it was too slow and unworthy. I told Terry that a record in the hand is worth two in the bush - the weather up there is very unpredictable and to take advantage of the opportunity he had - he could always bump it up later. Keenan, meanwhile, was having some ignition problems with his single cylinder Harley. The bike developed the nasty habit of melting the piston on nearly every run. This meant he either had to turn out or coast through the lights, depending on where on the track it happened. He finally qualified for a record at around 60, figuring I was right and he could always bump it up if the weather held.

I admit when Fritz first fired up our bike I was ecstatic - he'd been so tired while he was putting it together I didn't know if he had forgotten some minor detail, like say, the pistons. He always said he could build engines in his sleep. I guess this proved it. On our first run he qualified at 125 on a 122 record.

Andy and Ash eventually showed up driving Andy's Mustang II, which meant I could quit worrying about them. I, as usual, was acting as pit crew for all three of our group -Fritz, Terry and Keenan. We were in the pits talking and preparing to go out to the staging lanes when the subject of me being pit crew for all three of them arose. One guy hanging out with us looked at me and said, "Wow, you must be the Queen of Bonneville!" I liked the title - it's good to be queen. That may have been

182

the same year one of the nearby campers at Road's Bend, called me an 'earth goddess.' Okay, that one was a bit strange to me, but the thought was kind. I decided to stick to 'queen.'

In December of that year I was nominated to become the President of SDRC. At the meeting when that occurred I told Terry, "I'm both queen and president, and I still can't get my kids to clean their room."

He replied, "Obviously they don't understand the power you wield."

Daytona was a fun track...

Chapter 17

Swimming Pools and Racing Fools

It was the 1999 November El Mirage meet when I lost my '49 Ford. Not literally, but effectively nonetheless. I had made a pass down the track at about 105, and was being towed back to the pits by Andy in our '72 Chevy pickup at the return road speed of 15 mph. Keenan had run either right before or right after me, so he was being towed back at the same time. Through a miscalculation, he and his bike fell over between my race car and my tow vehicle. I slammed on the brakes and swerved to avoid him, and Andy, seeing what was happening, braked as well. The brakes in the Chevy were superior to the brakes in the '49, and I ran into the rear bumper of the truck, crumpling my fender, hood, and wiping out my radiator. The important thing, though, was I didn't run over my friend. Fritz always intended to help me repair the car, but soon it was relegated to the status of my '68 Cougar, which was still sitting in pieces. Both the Cougar, and the '49, became projects we would get to "someday." Occasionally on Mother's Day we would work on one or the other to placate me, but Fritz was easily distracted by other things that were more pressing to him and neither of my cars were ever finished.

Once in a while racing took a slightly different turn for us. For a few years we helped friends in the Great

Temecula Tractor Race, which was a small oval track race held once a year complete with mud hole. Fritz loaned his buddy Marty the flathead V8 from the roadster pickup to put in his '34 Ford truck, which bore the number 777. Obviously, the number was meant to be lucky, and I suppose in a certain way it was. Fritz was given the opportunity to drive the truck a few times during the races with Marty's wife Kim riding shotgun. I was in the stands filming when they got tangled up with another truck on the back straightaway, and flipped the truck. I turned off the camera to see better what was happening with my husband and Kim, who were basically fine thanks to decent seat belts. Fritz however, was annoyed that I hadn't gotten the whole thing on film, and wondered where my priorities were. Hmm. The following year Kim was called "Tumbelina", unless I'm confusing her with the truck's new nickname, and Fritz was nicknamed "Flipper."

Another time, Sharon, my boss at the garage where I was an automotive service writer, asked me if I could qualify her 1930 something John Deere Model B tractor for her. Sharon said she needed to be at the shop that day, but I'm not sure if she actually needed to work, or was just being kind and giving me an opportunity. After all, she was a particularly kind lady. I admit to a certain amount of trepidation operating a tractor that old and that large when I hadn't any previous experience of that nature. My other boss, her husband Dave, checked me out on it, and I agreed to give it a go. I didn't have to win. All I had to do was make it around the track twice, so Sharon could race the following day.

When it was time to race, however, I forgot about my trepidation. Even though I believe that tractor has a top speed of around six miles per hour, I was in it to win it. I got off the line first against the opposition, another lady on another slow vintage tractor. I managed to 'get wide' going through the mud hole, which wasn't that difficult given the size of the John Deere. Due to my skillful navigation, though, I didn't give the other driver a chance to pass me there. At least that's my story and I'm sticking to it. I hung on to a tenuous lead for both laps, keeping the inside lane, and repeating the same 'get wide' procedure in the mud hole the second time. I have to say, it was glorious. What a pity it didn't actually count for anything except qualifying.

In 2000, we decided to run nitromethane in the 1000 cc motor, both at El Mirage and at Bonneville. As Andy was lighter than Fritz, and an excellent rider, he got to be the jockey. Andy could probably write his own Bonneville stories. One of the problems with being the child of racers is if your birthday happened to fall during Speed Week, as his always did, you didn't have very many birthday parties growing up. The only one he ever had, in fact, was in 1994, when Speed Week was rained out. I would always take him a present and buy him a cake, but I felt like I was failing as a mother when it came to his birthday. While Andy was in impound on his 18th birthday, I mentioned to the tech inspector that I bought him a record for his birthday - okay, he did the riding, but I paid the entry.

The next year Andy started campaigning his own motorcycle, a 1000 cc Suzuki sport bike. He ran fairly consistently in the 160 to 164 range, which wasn't quite fast enough for a record. It was, however, fast enough to make setting one seem plausible. Enjoying his role as the hero rider, he pulled double duty, still riding the Harley for us as well.

Getting back to running nitro, it took us a few tries to figure out the jetting and fuel ratio, but I am a good chemist - I mixed the fuel - and Fritz was a gifted mechanic. It wasn't long until we became very successful this way, consistently running over 160 mph. Andy's top speed on the bike was at the September El Mirage in 2003, at a speed of 168.9 - not bad for a 1000 cc iron head Sportster with no fairing. Fritz also rode the Harley on occasion, but Andy, being lighter and more agile, was always just a little faster. These glory days lasted a few seasons, until finally the engine couldn't take the strain any more.

Since we had acquired this engine in a trade for a couple of old Dodge motors, we toyed with the idea of looking for another junkyard Sportster engine, but Fritz had already returned to his first love, the K Model. Since Andy was running the Sportster, Full House Mouse 2, in '03 Fritz decided it would be a good idea to put a sidecar on the Harley road racer, Old Black Magic, which still housed the KH. Side cars were becoming all the rage at El Mirage and Bonneville, and he wanted to venture into this venue. In my experience, a number of the people I knew who ran side cars, outside of the Dry Lakes, seemed a little crazy, and Fritz's decision did not alter my perception. We did set two records with it that year at Bonneville, both in side car vintage gas, and side car vintage fuel class.

As I've mentioned, when we went to Bonneville, it was never with the nice enclosed trailers that so many racers enjoy. Especially because we were always carrying a supply of junk yard gas with us, we had stuff crammed in and tied on everywhere - one time we got pulled over by a CHP on the way there because our plastic chairs tied on the back of the trailer were obscuring the license plate. We had some friends who commented they could always tell when we were coming because our rig looked like something out of "The Grapes of Wrath." They weren't far wrong -we did resemble the Okies of the dust bowl era with everything they could manage thrown in or on tied to their old vehicle.

We started taking artificial grass with us to use

as a ground cover, as race vehicles have to be parked over a tarp or some form of ground covering to protect the salt. We decided to take it a little further one year. I had a Mexican fan palm in a five-gallon container, so we brought that and a six-foot swimming pool. Bringing water in to the pool was its own challenge, but Andy managed that one. The pool idea worked fine except Fritz became the "Pool Nazi" and started yelling at everyone who used it if they weren't perfectly clean. This didn't set well with Andy, who had brought in all of the water to fill it, and wasn't particularly dirty, but got yelled at anyway. The situation further deteriorated when Keenan started washing parts in it. We had a pool for a few years there, sitting on our artificial grass, but I admit I was relieved when we stopped doing that. It was way too stressful trying to be peacemaker between the Pool Nazi and the kids.

The Pool Nazi in his natural element...

Chapter 18

A Star is Born

In March 2004, toward the end of my five-year tenure as SDRC president, I was honored along with three other female land speed racers as a 'Speed Queen' at a reception at the Petersen Automotive Museum in Los Angeles. While I was by no means the fastest woman there, I did enjoy myself, especially the question and answer session. The men asking the questions were primarily from El Mirage, so they were 'my people'. It's very good to be queen.

One of my duties as SDRC President was to conduct the meetings, which were held the first Thursday of every month. One such Thursday evening we were headed home from San Diego in our mostly green '72 Chevy pickup. The alternator had quit working some time earlier and Fritz hadn't replaced it yet, making sure the battery was fully charged before we went anywhere. With this in mind, he disconnected one headlight so the battery would last long enough to make it the 50 miles home. On our way into De Luz canyon, Fritz veered slightly across a double yellow line to take the left fork in the road. To our surprise, as there are few police out in our area, we were immediately pulled over by a county sheriff. Fritz, being old school, for lack of a better term, got out of the truck and began walking back toward the police car. The officer didn't like that plan, and told him to get back in his vehicle.

Fritz, with his hearing loss, couldn't understand and called, "What?" walking closer.

The deputy's voice sounded a bit more concerned as he again said, "Sir, get back in the vehicle!"

Fritz still couldn't make it out and said, "What??" again. He would have continued to go closer if I hadn't called out the window to get back in the truck. He said, "Oh", and got back in. Then he said, "Can we go now?"

Almost as exasperated as the sheriff, I said, "No!"

About this time the slightly nervous deputy cautiously approached the truck with his hand resting on his gun. I apologized that Fritz was hard of hearing. Fritz piped up and told him, "Back in the old days, people got out of their vehicles to talk to the police when they were pulled over."

The officer assured him that was no longer the correct procedure. Fortunately, my husband waited until the officer had walked back to his car to run Fritz's license to add he'd been doing that since before the deputy was born. I was glad he waited, because it probably wouldn't have gone over well. After he returned, somewhat mollified, but not entirely convinced, he informed Fritz of the reason for pulling him over. He said seeing him cross the double yellow line he thought perhaps Fritz had been drinking, which thankfully was not the case.

Fritz's response to this was, "Everybody out here crosses the double yellow on that corner."

The officer replied, "I don't."

Fritz answered, in an almost patronizing tone, "Oh. You haven't been out here long, have you?"

By this time the sheriff sounded almost defensive as he replied, "Yes I have!" Then, in a more assured voice he stated, "I've been patrolling this strawberry patch for a while now."

Now it was Fritz's turn to look unconvinced, so the deputy decided to try a different tack. He said, "Your registration is out of date," which it was, by a couple of days.

At that point it was my turn again, and I apologetically explained I had recently mailed payment to DMV and hadn't received the new registration yet. Accepting that, he tried one more time. "I noticed one of your headlights is out."

Fritz acted surprised, and remarked, "Oh, it is? I can get out and beat on the fender and see if it starts working again."

As he reached for the door handle, at this point the poor deputy had been through enough and said, "No! Just...go home!"

Fritz said, "Okay, thank you," and we headed down the road, me breathing a sigh of relief.

Jason began his racing career in 2004. He made his drag racing debut at Los Angeles County Raceway (LACR) in Pearblossom, riding the '53 Triumph Speed Twin. Fritz was a frequent winner in the motorcycle division, but this year Jason took that honor. None of the rest of our group did any good in our races, so Jim, who had also been eliminated, said that Jason was the only one in our group who was worth anything, although he expressed it more colorfully.

It was also in '04 that Jason first ran at Bonneville, on his '82 Honda CX500. He and Fritz both set records that meet, with Fritz on the Harley, of course. For several racing seasons, Chris, who had always been slender, crawled back and forth through the windows between the cab of the truck and the camper. Not only could he go in back when he was bored and wanted to take a nap, he was able to grab snacks and drinks for those of us who were less slender. After a few trips, though, one wall of the camper on the green monster started to compress, earning it the name, "Tilt'n Hilton." It was kind of like one of those mystery houses you see advertised, where one wall is slightly shorter than its opposing counterpart. Something feels off, but you aren't quite sure what, because logic tells you it shouldn't be that way. While at least we weren't losing yo-yos, it did begin to make Chris's travels between the cab and the camper more challenging, and this year's Speed Week was no exception.

Then, one day it happened. It had rained, and the dragged road between the blacktop and the pits was flooded. We left the pavement and were on the way out to our pit, driving through several inches of water on the slushy salt. Chris was trying to get something out of the back when he got stuck his head and arms in the camper, his backside and legs in the truck, and his poor little stomach trapped in the gap. He couldn't move either direction, but Fritz didn't think it would be prudent to stop in the slush, as there was the potential of getting stuck. He kept going toward the pits, having to drive slowly.

Poor Chris! He couldn't move either forward or backward, but he could reach a note pad and a pen, so he kept drawing sad faces and managed to pass them through the connecting window to me. We finally reached our pit and comparatively dry salt, where we decided the only way to extricate him was to push on the compressed side of the camper to try to relieve enough strain for him to escape. Warren, a fellow SDRC member and all around good guy, walked over and without a word started pushing too. After a bit he asked why we were doing this, which I explained. Luckily, with his help we were able to push hard enough for Chris to free himself. From that point on we had to plan ahead when we wanted cool drinks, and make them accessible without the risk of smooshing our youngest son.

Fritz and I were such an inseparable team that it

was odd to think of him going racing without me, but there were a several times he did. Our friend Jack had asked Fritz if he would help him time the first of Dennis Manning's motorcycle only events, named after his streamliner, BUB. Fritz had never been an official timer before, although he and I had helped Jack with a private meet for a streamliner at Bonneville a year or so before. Being a timer included setting up the clocks and calculating the elapsed time between them to determine the speed. Fritz enthusiastically agreed, with the provision that he would get to race the Harley when he wasn't working. My only problem with this was the dates of the event. The BUB meet was to be held at the beginning of September, right when school was starting for Jason and Chris. I hated being left behind, but had to be responsible. So, a week after we got home from Speed Week, Fritz left for the salt again, this time with Jack instead of me.

It worked out that he would be getting back from the BUB meet just in time for El Mirage, so we agreed to meet there. A number of people made comments about the salt falling off the truck - something to the effect that El Mirage was the wrong lakebed for that. Thanks to Jack, I had been able to get periodic updates from Fritz, including that he had made the first pass at the inaugural meet on our Harley, which truly meant a lot to him. Fritz would go on to set a record at that meet and at the subsequent BUB events. It was always one of the highlights of the year for him, especially once Jason was out of school and able to go with him.

While we were at Speed Week, some Hollywood people were there interviewing older racers, like Fritz, about Burt Munro. Burt was a Bonneville motorcycle racing legend from New Zealand, who had run back in the '60s and early '70s. I didn't think any more about it until after the BUB meet, when Jim L. called and asked Fritz if he wanted to take a couple of his bikes up to the salt for the filming of a movie about Munro in October. Jim also wanted Fritz to help him with some of the cars and bikes that he was taking, most notably, the Redhead streamliner. Fritz was in favor this, but as we were a team it was made clear that I would go as well, which meant taking Jason and Chris out of school for what I thought would be a week. Filming went slower than planned and one week turned into two. But as I told the office staff at both schools, how many times will my kids have the opportunity to make a movie with Anthony Hopkins? Besides, being at Bonneville and actually having a hotel room to go to at night with a real shower sounded like a wonderful novelty, especially when we didn't have to pay for it.

Before filming actually started, we had to sign up as extras, which meant we actually got paid to be there. Most definitely another novel experience. We met with director Roger Donaldson's assistant, April, as well as the casting director, and dealt with all the paperwork. Once at the salt, we were impressed with how well the movie crew had recreated the pits from 1962. We established our pit where they told us and helped unload some of our friend's cars. The crew loved our '72 Ford crew cab with the camper on it, which due to its partial collapse on one side, Fritz had labeled in big black letters on the back "Tilt'n Hilton". They were disappointed when we told them it was too new to use in the film, but agreed they had to be historically accurate. We were pleased to see our friends Jim and Randy with Mickey Thompson's Challenger, which doesn't often make public appearances, as well as their Pumpkinseed streamliner.

It was also totally cool to see the Flying Caduseus, which was on loan from a museum and extremely well protected. The museum was so concerned about the historic race car that they put it back in its container

194

and drove it off the salt every night. Weather is always a potential issue at Bonneville, and during the filming was no exception. After we had one of the freak storms that blow through there, the museum decided the risk to the Caduseus was too great, and pulled it off the set and took it back home. Fortunately for the film crew, they already had sufficient footage of the car and it didn't affect them too much.

Part of filming a movie is going to wardrobe. The wardrobe mistress took one look at Fritz's jeans, t-shirt and boots, and pronounced him perfect. Sixteen-year-old Jason had refused to cut his long hair, so she insisted that he wore it tucked up under a pith helmet to hide it. Chris's hair they decided to cut between takes- he wasn't seen enough to show the evolution of his haircut during the filming, which is probably just as well. There was one scene where he had to keep carrying a toolbox across the pits, and with every take his hair grew shorter. As for me, I remember my mother when I was a young girl wearing clothes like they gave me. Somehow, I think they looked better on her.

I'll never forget when Fritz met Sir Anthony. He said, "Oh Mr. Perkins, this is such an honor." Mr. Hopkins was a class act and just kind of looked at him and thanked him. Although Fritz was mortified when he realized what he had done, the rest of us thought it was quite funny. While Anthony Perkins was a fine actor - think Norman Bates in "Psycho" - he had passed away over a decade earlier. But in spite of Fritz's mistake, Sir Anthony - Hopkins, that is- seemed to like him, and would occasionally chat with him between takes.

The filming itself was an interesting experience, although there were things I most definitely didn't see as remotely probable until I saw the finished product. Some of the dialogue seemed extremely unrealistic at the time, but when I saw the movie it coalesced much better. Fritz had previous movie experience, dating all the way back to the late 60's when he helped with the B-25s in the iconic film "Catch 22", even getting a little 'stick time' in the process. More recently, he had been an extra in the Jason Priestly movie, "Calendar Girl", when we rented the movie company our '56 Ford Pickup and the '39 Ford coupe. Since he considered himself to be an old hand at this sort of thing, he knew what to expect. He did mention the food on the set of "Calendar Girl" was much better, even if the movie wasn't. Granted, I'm prejudiced in favor of "World's Fastest Indian", as I understand Burt Munro's motivation, having lived with Fritz. But as far as I was concerned regarding the food, it was two meals per day I didn't have to provide. Some evenings we got sandwiches from the nearby Subway, and sometimes it was food from the market. We didn't have a kitchen in our room, so I couldn't actually cook. We did buy 10 pounds of gummy worms that were on clearance, and snacked on them for the two weeks.

We didn't work on Sundays, so we went to the Wendover airport museum and checked it out. Wendover achieved notoriety during World War II when the Enola Gay was sent from there to bomb Hiroshima. While neither Fritz nor I were fans of nuclear devastation, we were, of course, fans of aircraft, and it was very interesting.

Fritz was always willing to help his friends with their race vehicles, and filming this movie was no exception. He helped Jim and Randy when they fired off the Pumpkin Seed, and Jim L. and Bill when they ran the Redhead. He was getting to be in so many shots that the director was beginning to take exception to it. Fritz, however, though it was great, and started referring to Sir Anthony as "my (Fritz's) co-star."

And then came his big scene, which unfortunately

ended up on the cutting room floor. Mr. Donaldson told Fritz to make a mock run, going down about 50 yards, and turn out. The stunt people were not happy with this arrangement, and I heard Roger assure them that Fritz knew what he was doing and was very professional. He didn't count on two things - first, that Fritz was inherently a racer, and putting him next to a black line on the salt would cause instinct to take over, and the second was Fritz was not above showboating a little. So, he took off, slightly pulling the front wheel off the ground in the process, and tore off down the track a good half mile. Roger watched him, turned around and said something to the effect of, "Well, I just lost my credibility." Take two went a bit more according to the director's plan, but as I said, they didn't use the scene in the movie anyway.

Chris's most prominent memory was that movie people didn't know how to put radiator caps on race cars. There were about seven people clustered around the car and none of them could get the radiator cap on, so 12-year-old Chris had to do it for them. When I asked Jason what he remembered the most, he said he remembered hiding out in our friend Elmo's pit. Elmo had been racing at Bonneville since before I was born, and knew it about as well as anyone could. The casting director called Elmo the "weatherman" and would frequently come to him for predictions, which as I recall were always right.

Jason also reminded me that the rear brakes locked up on the green monster in the middle of the salt. It took quite a bit of work to get the drum off and find the problem, and disable the brakes so we could move the truck. We had to order parts in town from Salt Lake, but being on the salt for two weeks, we had plenty of time. Fritz said it was mostly level in Wendover and we didn't really need rear brakes until we headed home, so he wasn't particularly worried about it.

Some of the extras had no clue of the value or historical significance of the machinery they were milling around. I remember one girl who decided to sit on the Challenger and pose. As I was about to make my way over to her and tell her to get her butt off of the car before Jim decided to pull it off the set, one of the director's assistants saw her and shooed her off. Luckily, no harm was done to the car. I realize she didn't know any better, but seriously, I felt honored when Jim let me help push it. Not many people get to touch that million-dollar piece of history. And had Jim been there and seen it, he would have had that car and the Pumpkinseed off the salt before you could say Anthony Perkins.

One of the funnier things that happened occurred while SCTA was putting on their event, World Finals, a short distance from where we were filming. Fritz had thought about trying to both work on the movie set and race, but chose to focus on the movie. I don't think he thought his 'co-star' could get along without him. One of the SCTA racers turned out after making his run, and headed for what he thought was the pits. The only problem was, he aimed for the wrong pits. He got to the movie set pit near us, where everything was 1962 - everything from the people to the race vehicles to the timing stand. Even the gas cans and tool boxes sitting in the pits were period correct. The poor guy seemed extremely confused for a moment - it was as though he'd gone back in time and entered "The Twilight Zone." Fritz naturally took advantage of the situation and undoubtedly messed with the guy a bit before finally relenting and explaining what had happened.

After two weeks of "Okay people, that was really good, but we're going to do it again. Everybody keep your energy up. Back to one!" (meaning back to where you started the scene) the director decided he had enough of

Bonneville, probably in more ways than one. We repaired the brakes on the truck, loaded the trailer, and headed back down the road.

When the movie was released and we went to the theatre to see it, I noticed people looking at Fritz afterward, realizing that he looked pretty familiar to them. He ate it up like candy - I was surprised he didn't want me to bring a stack of signed photos to pass out. Actually, I think he probably would have liked that - I just didn't have any handy.

A little time travel back to 1962

Chapter 19

Adversity with a Triumph

As spring arrived the following year, so did the racing season. El Mirage began in May, and the Antique Nationals was held in early June. This year Fritz managed to edge Jason out in the final round of the motorcycle division. I had the '39 Ford Coupe up there, and lost fairly egregiously early on. It was fun while it lasted, though.

I don't remember much about Bonneville itself in '05, but I do remember the trip home. We usually returned the way we came, through Alamo, as it was the shortest route. This year, though, we decided to go back through Caliente, as I hadn't been that way in 20 years. Shortly after leaving Ely, Fritz saw a cloud of dust that he knew meant a motorcycle rider had gone off the road. Immediately we pulled over, and he ran across and climbed down into the ravine where the man and his girlfriend were lying. Shortly after we stopped, another man pulled up behind us in his pickup. After learning what had happened, he quickly drove back up the mountain to where he had cell phone reception and called for help. While we were waiting for the ambulance to arrive, Fritz calmed and comforted the female passenger, who only had a few abrasions, and held the man in his arms, who had more serious injuries - encouraging him, being with him, telling him he was going to be okay. The ambulance eventually

200

arrived and we continued on toward home. Fritz could be pretty, shall we say, self-focused when it came to racing, but when it came to what really mattered, in this case a badly injured total stranger, he had a depth of compassion that is hard to find.

After passing through Caliente we decided to let Jason drive for a while. At this point the green monster had been to the salt so many times the exhaust was rusted through in places, with result being an extremely loud truck. We had to shout sitting next to each other just to have a conversation. He'd been driving a number of miles when he glanced in the rearview mirror and saw an ambulance directly behind him. He pulled over to let it pass, and we speculated about whether it was the man we had stopped to help, on his way to the hospital in Vegas. Immediately after the ambulance passed, a Nevada State Trooper pulled us over. He came to the window and told Jason that ambulance had been following him for at least a mile, and brusquely asked him why he hadn't pulled over sooner. Jason sincerely apologized and said he hadn't heard it because of the noise from the truck, nor seen it earlier because of the width of the camper. Fritz, in the front seat with him, explained the exhaust had failed at Bonneville and told him we were going to repair it when we got home. The officer was somewhat appeased, but asked to see Jason's license, which happened to be in the camper. I offered to go back and get it, since I couldn't send Chris through the window anymore. The Trooper was content to run Jason's social security number, which was available, and let us go with an admonition to be more careful.

A few weeks later, Jason decided to run the BUB meet with his dad. I wasn't convinced how well this would work with school, but I was outvoted by Fritz. Jason set a record on his Honda CX500, which to him was worth missing the first week of his junior year. His teachers probably had a wildly different opinion.

The following year, 2006, Fritz decided it might be an interesting experiment to run the side car at the Antique Nationals. This was not his best idea ever. The side car required plenty of room for a gradual turn out. This was no problem at El Mirage and Bonneville, but such was not the case at the drag strip. While making his way onto the return road after an elimination run, the bike refused to stay to the left and crashed into the fence. Fritz was injured in the incident, and was unable to continue racing that day.

For him to stop racing, he must have been in excruciating pain. I remember one Saturday evening at El Mirage when he was trying to kick start the Harley in his sandals, and it 'kicked back.' There was a loud popping sound as the tendon in his big toe on his right foot snapped, leaving it permanently stuck out at about a 30-degree angle to his foot. It hurt like heck, but he still stuffed it in his boot and ran the next day. Another El Mirage he was bitten by a black widow while we slept outside the night before the race. He felt terrible as the venom worked its way through his bloodstream, but still made one run before every muscle in his body cramped up so badly that we had to go home. He definitely wasn't one to give up easily.

In August Jason wanted to run BUB again, this time on his '05 Yamaha R6. Jason has a brilliant mind, but he wasn't particularly excelling in high school. We decided he could transition to a home school program his senior year, even though I had mixed feelings. He set another record that year, so it was still worth it to him.

Fritz still had the sidecar on the Harley. Unlike Speed Week and El Mirage, at the BUB meet human ballast was allowed. Fritz had engineered and built the sidecar especially for dry lakes racing, which meant it was in no way enclosed to reduce drag. It was basically a platform with a wheel, securely mounted to the bike in a couple of places. While thinking about ballast, he met Samantha, a friend of a friend. He walked behind her, put his hands on her waist and lifted her up to check her weight. Setting her down, he said, "You'll do." Once he actually explained what he was talking about, she eagerly agreed to be human ballast. She was a stunt rider who used to ride the "Wall of Death" for a living, or something along that line. Fritz would frequently rave about her in glowing terms, and even though Samantha gave me no cause for it, I admit to a bit of jealousy. It didn't help when Fritz told me I couldn't have done what she did even if I had been there - he said I was too heavy. I don't think he ever figured out why this wasn't an appropriate thing to tell his wife. The two of them went on to set a record or two on the Harley that meet. Even though I wasn't particularly thrilled with Fritz's incessant and effusive praise of her, I never held anything against Samantha. She was a nice woman who was brave enough and light enough to kneel on a platform holding on to a brace with one hand and with her other arm around my husband's lower back at 100 mph. For her sake, I was pleased it worked out as well as it did. She'd already broken enough bones in the course of her stunt riding career.

In 2007, we decided I should run our 1955 supercharged Triumph at Bonneville. This sounded good in theory, but the reality wasn't so great. I had made a pass at Bonneville a few years earlier in a friend's '38 Ford, with a speed of 136, so, combined with 20 or so years of experience as crew chief, I wasn't exactly a rookie at racing on the salt. My problem wasn't with running; it was with the bike in question. The clutch had some major issues, and while it wasn't a big deal to someone like Fritz who had been riding for 50 years, it was more of a problem for me, whose motorcycle experience was limited to desert riding and riding around the ranch. Well, aside from the time I dumped the Harley road racer while learning to ride it, that is. And come to think of it, I also laid down Keenan's Harley once at the drags, but that's a story for another time. Or perhaps it's best left untold.

But, back to Bonneville - he was frustrated with me, which he expressed loudly and frequently, especially at the starting line when I was getting ready to make a run. I was frustrated with the bike, because I knew I should be able to ride the silly thing. Other competitors were sensible enough to stay away from us when we were expressing our frustrations. I finally made a clean pass (down run) and was ready for my record run the next morning. We reached the salt nice and early, which is my favorite time of day there. Few things compare to watching the sun rise over the salt flats - the cool air, the colors, the excitement because you know you are there at that time for a reason.

When it was my turn to go, I took off cleanly from the line. This had been my whole issue with the bike - shifting and pointing it straight at 90 mph were no big deal. I was exhilarated - I thought I was finally going to make it. I had just gone through the two mile marker when the Triumph quit running. This was problematic, because the short course is three miles long, and you are timed between the two and a quarter and the three mile markers, with a subsequent shut down area. I coasted as far off the course as I could and had to push it the rest of the way through the damp salt to the return road, with the salt building up on the tires and my boots as I trudged onward. This build up made my boots heavier with every step, and increased the bike's resistance with every rotation of the wheels. By the time I was clear of the race course, I was extremely warm in my leathers, to say the least, and more than mildly irritated with that English piece of machinary.

When we finally got it back to the pits and looked at it, we realized the throttle cable had come out of the slide in the carburetor, effectively cutting off my fuel supply and my chances for a record. I had difficulties with the bike for the rest of that week - I was able to make down runs but never able to back them up with a return run. Frustrated with my inability to close the deal Fritz decided he had to do it for me, and set a record on the Triumph. He never got why this made me so angry, or why I never acknowledged that record. It had no meaning to me. It wasn't mine, it was another one of his, and he already had plenty - over the course of our racing efforts we set around 50 of them. Motorcycles were okay - well, maybe not that one at the moment, but the bottom line was I wanted my car back, even if it did have a sloppy steering box and no second gear.

I began to reminisce about the '49. I was always faster in my Ford than Fritz was able to be, both at El Mirage and at the drags. At one particular Antique Nationals, he decided he was going to show me how it was done, and was going to teach me how my car should be driven. When he couldn't beat, or even match, my time, I thought it was pretty darned funny, as did some of our friends. I know it seems petty, but I had to take my victories where I could find them. Upon further reflection, he never beat my time running the Lincoln at the drags either, although in his defense, my best run in it was at sea level at Carlsbad Raceway. After that track was shut down he was trying to beat my time under different conditions at a much higher elevation. Nonetheless, victory was sweet.

I wasn't always exactly the queen of drag racing, though. Driving the '49 during one elimination run at LACR in Palmdale, I over-staged, which meant I went too far past the staging lights and had to back up. I finally got appropriately staged, and when the tree came down (the lights changed from yellow to green) I went to dump the clutch and take off on the last yellow, only to realize I was in neutral. That was by far the slowest reaction time I ever had - three seconds may not sound like much in the course of normal events, but in drag racing it is an eternity. My reaction time was usually around three tenths of a second, which still isn't amazing, but I could work with it. Three seconds, however, is how long it took me to figure it out, jam it into first gear, and leave the line. Not exactly my finest moment, but at least I hadn't left it in reverse, which could have been pretty exciting for the car waiting to stage behind me. Ah, the good old days...

Fritz ran the Triumph at the May 2008 El Mirage meet. He called it "Hellzapoppin" after a B25 bomber, which is a nicer name than I would have chosen after riding it the previous summer. It was the '54 Harley that went to Bonneville that year, though. We raced the K Model with some success, setting a record in the partial streamline vintage gas class, and Jason ran his Honda CBR slightly less successfully. Fritz and Jason had decided before we left home they would stay at the salt between Speed Week and the BUB meet, as there was only a week in between the two. If felt strange to leave them there, but Jason's fiancé Sarah had to get back to her job, Chris was due to start school, and I had responsibilities to attend to as well.

They used the time between events to help with a private meet, and somehow adopted a field mouse. It slept with Fritz and ate holes in my sheets, not to mention their leather boots, once again fulfilling the team name, Full House Mouse Racing. He was their companion for two weeks, and Fritz would leave him with one of the girls in the registration trailer while he was racing.

At the end of the week, before they came home, Fritz set the little guy free in the city park. The BUB meet was successful for both of my races, as they each set a record, and enjoyed being night security. By the time they got home, they were so sunburned and otherwise burnt out from three weeks on the salt they decided, though, that perhaps it was a bit too long to stay up there.

"It's easy! Just let out the clutch!"

Chapter 20

Does Anyone Else Honeymoon at Bonneville?

Our lives revolved around racing, but there were other events in family life as well. In 2004, I miscarried twins, which devastated me. Around six weeks later, Andy got married to Sami, instantly gaining a son with her three-year-old, Justin. Zeke married his long-time sweetheart Georgi in 2009, and Jason and Sarah were married in 2010, which is also the year Sami and Andy had their daughter Michelle.

LA County Raceway was permanently closed around 2008, and the Antique Nationals was moved to Fontana. I was sad when that happened, as it was the end of an era. Every year, after a long day of racing, we would treat ourselves to date milk shakes at a little place in Pear-blossom, a few blocks from the track. I kept thinking of the song *"They paved paradise and put up a parking lot."* I think it became a gravel pit, not a parking lot, and few people would call the desert heat and wind paradise, but I missed it.

One year after the Antique Nationals had moved to Fontana, Jason decided to run the super charged Triumph. He had a whole new set of issues with it, including it not wanting to start and it throwing the blower belt. As angry as he and I have both been with that Triumph, it's a wonder that bike still exists. Perhaps if Fritz had any of his dynamite left from the '60's, it wouldn't.

Speed Week was always interesting. We were back to running the K Model with the twin aluminum tanks Fritz fabricated back in our 'nitro glory days' with the Sportster engine. The rules were constantly being revised for the good of the sport, and occasionally we either missed a change or misinterpreted the rule. In all fairness, at least one rule had been changed years earlier because of Fritz's strict interpretation of it, which was not actually the spirit of the rule. And sometimes, in our pre-Bonneville sleep deprivation, we would forget something. That being said, we always appreciated the rules that were put in place for the safety of the competitors, and did our best to comply with them.

One of the regulations for running fuel class was being able to shut off the flow of fuel without removing your hands from the controls. The way I remember it, a fellow competitor pointed out a problem with our system to the head tech inspector, for our own good I'm sure. It couldn't have had anything to do with the fact he was running in our class and we were known for setting records. Nonetheless, the inspector agreed with him and rules are rules, so we had to come up with a different way to follow them, using what was available to us at the time. Fritz drilled a hole through the end of the handle of our fuel shut off valve, and attached a bungee cord to it. He wrapped the other end of the bungee around his leg. All he needed to do was move his right knee away from the motorcycle, and the ball valve would close. He demonstrated its effectiveness to the inspector, blandly calling it a "standard knee lanyard," like everybody should know what that was.

The inspector, who was a good guy, kept a straight face and said something to the effect of, "Okay, that's fine, it works." I did wonder how many 'standard knee lanyards' he had come across, but wisely didn't ask.

The other competitor wasn't entirely happy, as it was not a conventional solution. Then again, Fritz was not a conventional man, and it was an effective solution. Such is racing.

It reminded me of another time when someone running in our class whined about our foot pegs being measured incorrectly from the axle. This put us in the wrong class, which also disallowed the record we had just set. That was a genuine misinterpretation on our part, as we were measuring diagonally, not laterally. After being told by the inspector we were mistaken, we adjusted the position of our axle, which moved our foot pegs the required three eights inch to be legal for the class we were running. We headed out to the line to requalify, and set a record at a much higher speed than we had the day before. I think there is probably a moral in that story somewhere, but I'm not quite sure what it is.

I was finally able to go to the BUB meet with Fritz in 2009. It was odd that it was just the two of us - no kids for once. He called it our second honeymoon, and since our first had also been spent at Bonneville, I couldn't disagree. We were night security, which was a new experience for me. I had never been allowed to spend the night on the salt before, and it took on an almost mystical quality in the cool evening air. The stars were shining like jewels in the velvet black sky, and the cloudy looking Milky Way Galaxy wove its way through the heavens. The atmosphere was very conducive to rekindling a romance that had begun at Bonneville 24 years earlier. Occasionally, racers would ask permission to stay a little later to prepare for the next day, but in general it felt like we were alone on a desert island.

Of course, there are always exceptions. Around midnight early in the week we heard a vehicle out near the timing tower. Since the salt was officially closed and no one else was supposed to be there, we prepared to go after them, which merely meant getting dressed and folding up the steps on the camper. Like the green monster before it, our trusty rusty '71 Ford had gotten a bit on the loud side after multiple trips to the salt had eaten holes through the exhaust system. When we pulled out of the pits to chase down the vehicle and tell them they weren't supposed to be there, we apparently scared them half to death. They heard us roaring in their direction and took off toward the pavement and civilization like the hounds of hell were after them.

I discovered racing itself was conducted somewhat differently than at Speed Week, so I had to relearn being pit crew. One of the first things I noticed was we didn't wait in line, we were in a 'que'. It was the same thing, but it sounded much classier, and I think the wait times were shorter with the way it was structured. There were also different return run procedures, which were in some ways reminiscent of the early days of Speed Week. We had completed a qualifying run and were preparing to make our return record run going the opposite direction. It was our turn when the Harley decided it didn't want to start, and Fritz, in his black leathers, was attempting to kick start it to the point of heat exhaustion. Luckily for us, near us in the que were some lovely people who were using a Rolls Royce as a pit vehicle, and they had a set of rollers. The purpose of rollers is to turn the rear wheel while the bike is in gear, and thus start the engine. I don't know how many other people can say they have had their Harley started by a Rolls Royce, but it worked quite nicely for us. Thanks to them, Fritz was able to make his return run and achieve his record.

One of the highlights of the week was hanging out with the Buell Brothers and Sisters Race Team at the end of each race day. There was 'Old Style' beer and lots of good cheese that Santa Claus had brought with him from Wisconsin. In case you are wondering, yes, I do know Santa and he's a great guy. Sometimes either 'Indian Joe' or Horst or Drew would play guitar and sing, and there was always some good bench racing happening. I could easily see why Fritz was so fond of these people and spoke so highly of them. Fritz had his share of disagreements with tech inspectors throughout the course of his racing career, but he had the utmost respect for Drew, the singing chief inspector. When I think of the expression 'good people', I think of all of them.

At the end of that meet, Fritz was surprised and honored to win the 'Enthusiast of the Year' award put on by the Buell Brothers and Sisters. Being honored by his peers in that way brought tears to his eyes. It had been an amazing week spent with amazing people, and I could see why the BUB meet meant so much to him.

We ran El Mirage the following year, but the May meet was the only time Jason ran. He was accused of breaking a rule that he didn't break, and it didn't sit well with him that he was being ostracized for something he didn't do. Fritz frequently skated on the edge of the rules; in fact, as I've said, I can think of several that were modified directly because of his interpretation of them. I, however, am a bit more conservative when it comes to following the rules. Since Jason takes after me in that respect, the incident definitely irritated him.

At the end of that summer Fritz and I went to the BUB meet again, only this time Jason and Chris were able to go with us. It was Chris's first time at BUB, but I know he thoroughly enjoyed it as much as the rest of us. Looking at my sons, and missing Andy and Zeke, it was hard to believe they were already grown. It seemed like yesterday that baby Jason was playing with his dad's tools in Mexico, and baby Chris was a cranky two-month-old I was trying to keep cool on his first trip to the salt. Now Jason was setting records of his own, and Chris was pushing his dad on the Harley as he left the starting line. I realized I'd watched my family grow up on the salt. There is something about Bonneville, as inhospitable and unpredictable as it may be, that will always be home to my family.

"Dad, have you been gaining weight?"

Diary of a Racer's Wife

Epilogue

August, 2012

It's been a little over a year since Fritz passed away, and the first time I've been to Bonneville without him since we met there 27 years ago. He had a massive heart attack in June, 2011 while helping Chris work on his '53 De Soto, trying to get it ready for the Antique Nationals. He died in my arms, and my name was the last word on his lips. Chris began dealing with his grief by going to the Antique Nationals a few days later, although the car was unfinished, and proceeded to win the motorcycle division on what is now his '53 Triumph Speed Twin. It reminded me of all those years ago when Fritz and I went racing in Mexico a few days after his father died. My family missed Bonneville the year we lost Fritz, as I was still stuck in my grief, and Jason and Andy were both expecting babies late that summer - Jason's first, a son; and twin girls to add to Andy's growing family. A few months later, Fritz was posthumously honored with a life time achievement award at both the SCTA banquet and at the Dry Lakes Hall of Fame, which is something he always secretly wanted. I was sorry he wasn't there to see it; he would have been so proud. Jason, Chris and I all felt the need to return to the salt, though, so I sold Fritz's '60 Chevy truck - the one he was driving when we met - to finance the trip. We decided to run the BUB meet. I cried when the organizers told me they had permanently retired Fritz's number, 408, unless the boys or I wanted to run it. We put Chris, who is much lighter, on Jason's Honda CBR600RR for his first timed journey down the salt. We called it 'Full House Mouse 3' as a tribute to their dad, my husband. The engine is a little tired, but Chris turned just over 150 on his second pass. I'm very proud. The legacy continues.

The Full House Mouse race team:
Zeke, Gayle, Fritz, Andy, Chris, Jason

Rudy, Fritz, and Junior at Model T hill climb

Before it became a theme park,
grownups used to play here...

"The Happiest Baby in Mexico"

Another example of training your pit crew at an early age
In this case, Chris

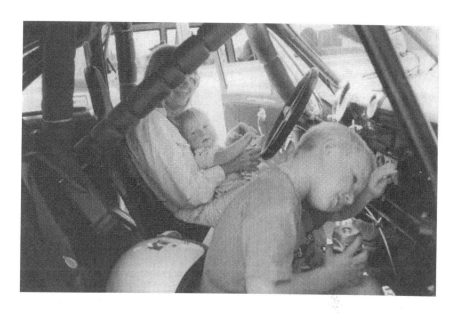

Normal life for my kids...

My poor boy!
It gives new meaning to 'torn between two worlds'

Andy satisfied with his record run

...Maybe I should have told him most people take the whole bike to impound to get certified...

The family that races together stays together...

Glossary

(Definitions by Gayle,

not Webster)

AHRMA: American Historic Racing Motorcycle Association. A racing organization which is lots of fun with many lovely people.

BNI: Bonneville Nationals Incorporated. The sanctioning body for Bonneville Speed Week and the Bonneville World Finals.

Brodie: Spinning a vehicle half way around - it can be described as either half a donut or doing a 180 with flair.

Christmas Tree: The staging lights found at drag strips. Traditionally starts with three descending yellow lights followed by either green or red, depending on whether or not you leave the starting line too soon. Comfort can be attempted by telling those who 'red light' that they are just faster than electricity. The efficacy of this depends on their distress level and temperament. (FYI: pro trees are different - just simultaneous yellows to green/red, but are not in my range of experience.)

Clutchitis: A made up word referring to our vehicle's clutch not being completely fried, but close enough that it wouldn't be prudent to drive it. Although that certainly didn't keep us from driving the VW home from Florida.

El Mirage: A dry lake bed in California's Mojave Desert. SCTA holds speed trials there six times per year, weather permitting.

False Start: In reference to the La Carrera Classic, a parade through downtown Ensenada complete with an overhead banner advertising the race, cheering crowds, and a guy with a green flag to send off the racers. As long as you didn't get lost, or have your arm dislocated by all the kids wanting to give you 'high fives,' you would then proceed to the actual start of the race outside of town, where there was much less fanfare.

Impound: A designated area where return runs are awaited, engines are measured, and records are certified. My version of "the happiest place on earth."

La Carrera Classic: A shorter version of the Mexican Road Race, held between Ensenada and San Felipe in Baja California.

La Carrera Panamericana: The Mexican Road Race, held originally in the 1950's as a grueling all out race. It ran from the Guatemalan border to the Texas border. The organizers of the La Carrera Classic began running a modified version in 1988. Still grueling, but with different parameters.

Lakester: Specially constructed dry lakes car that has no fairing or covering of the wheels and tires. They are often really fast.

Marbles: Gravel and bits of rubber that build up on the outer edge of a race track or highway, which can be very slippery.

Pit Crew: The friends/ family of the hero rider/ driver who do everything they can, usually within the limitations of the rules, to ensure the success of their team.

Pits: The temporary home of the race vehicle while at the event. In my case, a good portion of my adult life was spent there. I have a wildly different idea than most people of a 'second home'.

Ported and relieved: Ported - the ports have material (cast iron) removed to allow for more and smoother flow of the air/fuel mixture. Relieved - an art form involving removing material from within the combustion chamber on a flathead block, and smoothing the area between the valve pockets and the cylinder, without messing up the compression. These two processes in tandem make a basically inefficient engine far more efficient. If you do it well, it works great. If you don't, well, overhead valve engines are easy to work with...

Record: Achieving a certified faster speed than anyone else in your class, which is the primary purpose of land speed racing. The opposite of beating your head against the wall.

Record Run: BNI and BUB records are based on the average of two runs over the same relative mile, although certain requirements are different for those two events.

Return Road: As implied, it is the designated road created to return the participant either to the pits, or, if they are fortunate, impound.

SCTA: Southern California Timing Association. The sanctioning body of El Mirage time trials, and parent organization of BNI, comprised of twelve clubs.

SDRC: San Diego Roadster Club. One of the member clubs of SCTA, founded in 1941. I was honored to be its first woman president.

Speedster: In this case, a Model T with a body built to be light weight, thus increasing the power to weight ratio. When one is dealing with marginal horsepower, every little bit helps.

Staging: Preparing to run on the designated course. In drag racing, this involves being in the correct position on the track, as denoted by the yellow staging lights. In Dry Lakes racing, this involves waiting in line for your turn, but being prepared to run - helmet on, seatbelts fastened, etc., three race vehicles back from the starting line. In road racing, it involves being where you are supposed to be, i.e. the hot pit, when you are supposed to be there, ready to race.

Streamliner: Land speed car or motorcycle constructed specifically for all out speed. Car classes must have 4 wheels, with at least two covered. Motorcycle classes must have two covered wheels leaving a single track, with the exception of side car streamliners, and be powered by one or two motorcycle engines. The fastest streamliner I have personally witnessed set a record at over 400 mph. It was most definitely something to see.

Technical Inspection: Process before a race during which the vehicle's and driver's safety equipment are inspected. One rule that I learned early - always be kind and polite to tech inspectors. They are concerned with keeping you alive, and deserve respect. Also, they can make your life miserable, if you annoy them too much.

TT: Tourist trophy. A motorcycle event comprised of twists and turns and hills. I liken it to primitive moto-cross, without the tabletops, although there are those who would doubtless vehemently disagree with me, including those who race the Isle of Man, the granddaddy of all TTs.

World's Fastest Indian: An awesome movie starring Anthony Hopkins. You should watch it.

Acknowledgements

Thank you to my children, Ezekiel, Andrew, Jason and Christopher, who always supported me, even when they didn't necessarily understand me. Thanks also to my daughters-in-law, Georgie, Sami and Sarah, for loving me, but more importantly, for loving my sons and my grand-children.

Thank you to my friend Jill Iversen, for your extremely valuable insights and editorial comments. You are a true racer, a brilliant writer, a treasured friend, and I am grateful beyond measure.

Thank you to my sweet Alyssa Kascak, a beautiful, talented daughter who has blessed me with her insights and her practical skills. You have been a light shining in the darkness, and I appreciate you more than you will ever know.

Thank you to my friend Jet Attardo - amazing artist, faithful supporter, and adopted daughter. Your help has been invaluable to me.

Thank you to my friend Peggy Collins, who encouraged me to keep writing. I heard once that a real friend is someone who sees you for who you are and likes you anyway. Thank you for being that friend, and seeing the real me. You are very dear to me.

Thank you to my parents, George and Mary Jane Wendland. Dad, you took me to my first race, and you taught me the value of patience and perseverance. Mom, you never wanted to know about our racing adventures until they were over, but you still enjoyed reading

1

about them. I always tried to write things I wouldn't be ashamed to have you read, and I still do. Also, thanks to my brothers and sisters: Jim, Karyn, Sally, Tom and Connie, who looked after me and loved me as their little sister. Connie, thanks for your prayers - I've needed them. Sally, you not only introduced me to Fritz and subsequently to the world of Dry Lakes Racing and beyond, but you entrusted your life to me in the midst of it a couple of times. You're very brave.

Finally, thank you to the racing communities I have been privileged to know. All y'all are good people.

77519162R00133

Made in the USA
San Bernardino, CA
24 May 2018